D0815535

Praise for *Not Alone*

Nell Noonan's book is magnificent. Magnificent because it's real, it's human, it's scriptural, it helps.

The Right Reverend Sam B. Hulsey
Bishop of the Episcopal Diocese of Northwest Texas, Resigned

Not Alone: Encouragement for Caregivers is a much-needed book for the growing number of caregivers in our society. Nell Noonan speaks out of her experience, caring for her husband, and the pages of this devotional book are full of meaningful thoughts for all caregivers. A cursory glance at the Contents points to the daily challenges that caregivers face but also the joys that can accrue from caring for a loved one. Nell Noonan is realistic about the endless burden of the thirty-six-hour day for caregivers and offers a spiritual support that provides incredible strength. I will have no hesitancy in making caregivers whom I serve aware of this book.

Richard L. Morgan
Author, Facilitator of Alzheimer's Support Groups

How much Nell's meditations would have helped those of us who cared for my friend and my mother! Her approach has the authenticity that comes from personal experience. It does not sugar-coat the harsh realities with maudlin sentimentality but addresses them head-on and realistically with a profound spirituality.

On behalf of all of us who have been or will be caregivers (and sooner or later that will be almost all of us), thank you, Nell, for this supportive and redemptive book.

The Reverend Canon William D. Nix Jr.
Canadian, Texas

As primary and only caregiver to my husband and my ninety-three-year-old mother, I know how badly caregivers need encouragement and how forgotten we are. Nell Noonan has created a wonderfully written series of uplifting reflections on the caregiving experience. She guides us to follow along the spiritual path she took to share her burden with Christ and receive strength from him. The stories became a companion when I needed peace and calming. I want to gift this book to every caregiver I meet. Thank you, Nell, for the dedication you've shown all caregivers in writing *Not Alone*, the affirmation of our good work, mercy when we've been not so good, and courage to keep trying.

Marilyn Stapleton
Retired teacher and research scientist

Wow! A must read for anyone who cares for another. This book is written from the depths of the soul of one who has lived the life of a caregiver. Jesus' mandate for us is simple, that we are to love and care for one another. That is great for the one receiving the love and care. But what about the caregiver—overlooked in the maze of helping and caring? Nell's words echo another great biblical theme—you are never alone! Her words will bring comfort, hope, and encouragement to the often forgotten caregiver.

The Reverend Randy Wild
Senior Pastor, St. Barnabas United Methodist Church

God does not always spare us from the storm, but God always walks with us in the storm. Nell Noonan has reminded us that God's blessings can be found even in the midst of very difficult circumstances. *Not Alone* will bless you.

The Reverend Dr. Scott Youngblood
Senior Pastor, Trinity United Methodist Church
Arlington, Texas

NOT ALONE

ENCOURAGEMENT *for* CAREGIVERS

NELL E. NOONAN

UPPER ROOM BOOKS®
NASHVILLE

The Upper Room® Web site: www.upperroom.org

UPPER ROOM®, UPPER ROOM BOOKS® and design logos are trademarks owned
by The Upper Room®, a Ministry of GBOD®, Nashville, Tennessee. All rights reserved.

Unless otherwise indicated, scripture quotations are from the New Revised Standard Version Bible, copyright 1989, Division of Christian Education of the National Council of the
Churches of Christ in the United States of America. Used by permission. All rights
reserved.
Scripture quotations marked NIV are taken from the HOLY BIBLE, NEW INTERNA-
TIONAL VERSION®. NIV®. Copyright 1973, 1978, 1984 by International Bible Soci-
ety. Used by permission of Zondervan. All rights reserved.
Scripture quotations marked RSV are taken from Revised Standard Version of the Bible
copyright 1952 (2nd edition, 1971) by the Division of Christian Eduction of the National
Council of Churches of Christ in the United States of America. Used by permission. All
rights reserved.
Scripture quotations from the King James Bible are noted KJV.

Permissions continued on pages 318–320.

Cover design: TMW Designs
Interior Design: Charles Sutherland
Second Printing: 2009

Library of Congress Cataloging-in-Publication
Noonan, Nell E.
Not alone : encouragement for caregivers / Nell E. Noonan.
p. cm.
Includes bibliographical references.
ISBN 978-0-8358-9982-6
1. Caregivers—Prayers and devotions. I. Title.
BV4910.9.N66 2009
242'.4—dc22   2008051573

Printed in the United States of America

With gratitude beyond words
I dedicate this book to two remarkable men of prayer:
my husband, Bob Noonan, and
my spiritual director, the Right Reverend Sam Hulsey.

They value me even in my scruffiest moments.
I am blessed.

CONTENTS

Tears and Laughter

Exhaustion and Resurrection

FOREWORD

Nell Noonan has provided a monumental resource for all of us through her book of daily meditations for caregivers. She knows of what she speaks, and her topics typify the up-and-down days of care receivers and their caregivers. The scriptural references are a great help.

Not all of us are cut out to be caregivers. Particularly in our culture, most people never thought they would be called upon the way they are. The lessons to be learned are amazing. Men and women have strengths they never dreamed of, but there is plenty of inadequacy and guilt to go around. For so many, the task lasts way too long. For those dealing with Alzheimer's, it truly is "the longest good-bye."

Deeply into my wife Linda's Alzheimer's, near the end of what I thought was a quite productive day, I said, "I've gotten so much done." She replied, "You're just Jesus' little friend." I felt honored, amused, and humbled.

Truly Jesus is the caregiver's friend with his gifts of acceptance, forgiveness, hope, and ever new beginnings. The tasks, the worries, and the process often feel endless, but the source of strength and compassion, for both the caregiver and care receiver, is also endless. This book reminds us of that over and over again.

The Right Reverend Sam B. Hulsey

ACKNOWLEDGMENTS

This book brings together scripture, prayer, and the experiences of a caregiving pilgrimage that both challenges and blesses. The influence and encouragement of many people are reflected in it. I extend profound gratitude to the members of the Freelance Writers Network of Fort Worth. They challenged me to become a better writer and to seek excellence in my written words. Linda Austin and David Walker were especially helpful with reading and critique. Kristen Lamb edited almost all these meditations while encouraging me to raise the standards of my writing.

The Right Reverend Sam Hulsey also read and commented on the devotions. He shared his own caregiving experiences, recommended resources, and directed me to the second group of remarkable people who had a huge impact on this project—the Alzheimer's support group that meets on Thursday mornings at First United Methodist Church of Fort Worth. They welcomed me, allowed me to share their stories, and became my mentors.

I am fortunate to have a team of women who encourage me to stretch, dream, and take on projects like this one. My beautiful cheerleaders include my mother, Nell Bass Eubanks; my sister, Dr. Mary W. Eubanks; my daughter, Elizabeth Schoenfeld; my soul friend, Emily Williams; and my agent, Etta Wilson. I would be remiss if I did not acknowledge the excellent technical support I received from Jack Jarrett. He always came through for me.

This book would not have been possible without the love and complete support of my husband, Bob. He is the project's hero.

To all of the above, my deep and abiding thanks. I could not have done it without you. And to God be the glory. Amen.

INTRODUCTION

Millions of children, parents, and spouses care for the impaired and chronically ill. The number grows as baby boomers hit their sixties and people live longer. These caregivers need inspiration and encouragement for the demanding journey of daily attending to a loved one or friend.

The caregiver's situation lends itself to isolation, sadness, and abdicated personal needs. I am the healthy spouse of a chronically ill mate. I do not know how I would survive without my daily time of scripture study, meditation, and devotional reading. A few years ago, I began to imagine how helpful I would find a book of devotions that delved into the emotions, concerns, and challenges of being a caregiver. One cold morning in January 2007, I reached an overwhelming awareness that the time had come to stop entertaining the wish for a caregiver's devotional book to better satisfy my needs. I stared into the dancing flame of the candle on the table next to my armchair and felt an urgency to begin writing.

A few days later I spoke with my spiritual director and friend, the Right Reverend Sam Hulsey. He lost his first wife to Alzheimer's and cofacilitates a support group for caregivers. When I described the project, he looked at me, eyes glistening, and said, "I am getting tingling sensations. This book is needed." With those words of benediction and his promise to companion me through to its completion, I began to write.

These devotions are based on real-life experiences—mine and those of other caregivers met during this pilgrimage. Names were changed in many cases for purposes of confidentiality and anonymity. A key learning for us has been the need to take care of ourselves. Among the 50 million people caring for a family member or friend in the U.S., the work takes an enormous toll. Research studies document that caregivers stand at risk for a host of mental and physical illnesses, many of which have roots in exhaustion, stress, and self-neglect. One article stated a caregiver loses an average of ten years of life expectancy.

The thought of reaching out for help simply does not occur to many who care for a debilitated person. Some consider getting help a sign of weakness or shirking their duty. Friends and family often don't realize what is going on and may be unsure about when to step in or what to do. Many caregivers use a toxic coping mechanism when they quash emotions smoldering beneath the surface. Caregiving is driven by empathy, love, and devotion, but these dear people often experience sadness, rage, frustration, guilt about their feelings, despair, and depression. Caregivers need assistance from friends, family, church, support groups, and professionals. We cannot go it alone. We need to discover ways to connect with others.

Critical to caring for ourselves is to understand our experience as a spiritual pilgrimage. God is with us in the tears and the laughter, the brokenness and the blessings, the exhaustion and the whispers of resurrection. Writing this book has taught me that when we pause daily to listen to our lives, God is there. The Great Divine Heart loves and cares. We are not alone.

Each devotion has three parts: scripture, personal experience, and prayer. Use these devotions daily to massage your spirits. I will pray that your ministry may bless you and foster a calm reverence for God's calling.

Brokenness and Blessings

The LORD *is near to the brokenhearted,*
and saves the crushed in spirit.

Psalm 34:18

1

Twelve-Minute Forever

—⊗⊗⊗—

Scripture Reading: 2 Corinthians 4:16–5:1

*For we know that if the earthly tent we live in is destroyed, we
have a building from God, a house not made with hands,
eternal in the heavens.*

2 Corinthians 5:1

I stood at the stove frying bacon. Intuition warned me something
was wrong when my husband walked behind me and suddenly
stopped. I turned, and he appeared frozen. His face was ashen;
he could not speak. Then he began to tremble, and the trembling
quickly developed into shakes, then convulsions.

I am not sure how I did it, but I managed to get down under
him with his body across my back. Instinctively I knew to hook
a chair with my foot and pull it over so that I could maneuver
Bob into it to break his fall and prevent head injury. It took all my
strength to inch my two-hundred-pound husband across the
kitchen as the convulsions grew more vigorous. I braced him in
the chair with my body, reached for the phone, and dialed 911.

The operator's voice broke the sense of helplessness and isolation. I gave her the address and described Bob's condition. She
asked whether we had pets; if so, I should put them up and then
unlock the door while she remained on the phone. By this time, Bob
was no longer convulsing. It was worse; he had gone totally limp.

I left Bob and followed the instructions. When I got back to
the phone, the operator said the emergency team was on the way.

I expressed deep thanks as I listened to the sirens of the fire truck and ambulance grow louder. Six men dashed through the front door. Everything felt surreal as if we were moving on fast-forward. I watched the team stretch Bob out on the floor and quickly hook him up to various pieces of equipment. They asked questions about his history and read the medical directives and list of meds I retrieved from my purse.

Bob appeared dead—sickly white, eyes rolled back, mouth open, motionless. The EMTs patted his hands and face. They repeated his name attempting to rouse him, but he remained unresponsive. I stood there "forever," thinking my love was gone—just like that—gone. Later, at the hospital, I learned "forever" was twelve minutes before his eyelids fluttered and he began to move.

Prayer: Lord God, Divine Healer, thank you for the incredible people who come to help us in our crises. More than anything else, we thank you for the blessed assurance that no matter what happens here on earth, each of us has an eternal home in your heart. Amen.

2
Not for Sissies

———

Scripture Reading: Psalm 146

*Praise the LORD, O my soul! . . .
I will sing praises to my God all my life long. . . .
The LORD lifts up those who are bowed down. . . .
Praise the LORD!*

Psalm 146:1b, 2b, 8b, 10c

Caregiving is not for sissies. Life is made up of tough and tougher stuff. No one understands that better than a person taking care of an invalid. Today I am learning praise is not for sissies either.

The whole notion of prayers of praise seems silly and naïve right now. I am watching my beloved slowly decline in body, mind, and spirit. My mental state has become sluggish from being homebound too long. My body aches from lifting my husband in and out of his wheelchair. I am sleep deprived from getting up several times during the night to check on him. The only phone call today was a reminder of tomorrow's doctor's appointment. I am tired, sad, bored, and not thankful.

Today is bitterly cold. For several hours an icy mix of snow and sleet has been falling. As I sit in my robe of self-pity watching from within a safe, warm, clean home, a childhood memory pops into my head. The first freeze meant the family got mugs of steaming hot chocolate topped with generous handfuls of marshmallows.

In a matter of minutes my husband and I are savoring the warmth and sweetness of that childhood treat. Each sip melts my gloom and brings a growing awareness of my blessings. The list is unending: breath, family, comfort, faith, food, friends, forgiveness, extravagant grace. . . .

It grates on my sensibilities when someone exhorts me with scripture about praising God at all times in all circumstances. If she would simply suggest I fix a big mug of Swiss Miss smothered with mini marshmallows, then I might get the message. Praise and gratitude cannot be far behind. You see, praise does not require submission. It requires awareness.

When I release whatever disturbs, worries, concerns, and upsets me and look at the deeper reality of my circumstances, something happens inside me. I notice, and then I start to say a prayer of praise for those good things taken for granted but forgotten in the midst of daily challenges.

———————

Prayer: Gracious God, thank you for the little things that can comfort us, like a mug of hot chocolate. And thank you for the moments when we glimpse the good things in our lives. Amen.

3
The Meds

—⊶⊷—

Scripture Reading: Ezekiel 47:6b-12

Their fruit will serve for food and their leaves for healing.
Ezekiel 47:12, NIV

This was supposed to be a day with a clear schedule to give me time to write. Those plans were once again preempted. I feel frustrated after spending the entire morning taking Bob to the clinic and the pharmacy. The annoying thing about the whole situation was not being able to prevent it.

A nightly news report informed us one of Bob's medicines could be responsible for a 43-percent increase in heart problems. Bob called the doctor's nurse the next day. Before he could state the reason for his call, Barbara said, "I bet you saw the TV program last night about the medicine you are taking. Come in to the doctor tomorrow morning and get it changed." I understand Bob's heart is more important than my writing, but I'm chapped about it anyway.

The neurologist put me in charge of my husband's medicines several years ago. I recognized this responsibility as vital to Bob's health, but I never guessed how tremendously time-consuming it would be. Every Tuesday morning, I fill the seven-day compartmentalized pillboxes—a clear one for morning and a blue one for evening. I also order the medicines we need refilled.

Twice a day, before breakfast and prior to dinner, I take a small tray and line it with a napkin. On it I set the glucometer kit, alcohol swabs, a syringe, the insulin bottle, a pill cup filled with meds, and one-third of a banana. A metal plate in the back of Bob's throat makes swallowing difficult, and he has discovered that placing pills in soft banana facilitates getting them down.

If we are going to be away from home at med time, we take everything, including a banana, with us. A small cooler with cold pack holds the insulin. I feel like I have revisited the stage of motherhood when my babies required cumbersome diaper bags.

Medicines exert significant impact on moods. When a drug or dosage gets changed, it takes days to regain the equilibrium. Recently Bob began a new medicine that caused a terrible red rash. Back we went to the doctor to get a medicine for the rash. An increase in pain med makes Bob fall asleep at the dinner table. I am reminded of a mobile: when one part is touched, all parts have to adjust—caregivers included.

Over the years the med routine has become a meaningful ritual I no longer resent, except when it interferes with my writing time. I have learned to pray for the well-being of my husband's body and soul each time I prepare a med tray.

Prayer: Almighty Father, the scriptures in Ezekiel and Revelation describe the trees on the riverbanks in the New Jerusalem. They have leaves for the healing of the nations. Thank you for the medicines of Love, Grace, and Hope that can make us healthy and whole. Amen.

4
Equity

‑‑‑‑‑ ⬡ ‑‑‑‑‑

Scripture Reading: Psalm 98

*Let the hills sing together for joy
. . . for he is coming
to judge the earth.
He will judge the world with righteousness,
and the peoples with equity.*

Psalm 98:8-9

Some months ago I began to search for ways to get my husband out of the house and more involved with people. Bob accepted my invitation to accompany me when I deliver Meals on Wheels. He is in charge of handing me chocolate candies to give our clients (sugar-free for diabetics) and dog treats for their tail-wagging companions.

Today we completed our deliveries, dashed home for a quick lunch, and drove twenty miles to the neurologist, arriving in time for my husband's appointment. We sat in the waiting room more than an hour—Bob nodding off to sleep and me knitting preemie baby caps for a local hospital. It was a long wait and a real downer. Instead of the mad rush, we could have slowed down to a normal pace all day.

The doctor and his staff were amazed at the improvement in Bob's health over the past three months, and Bob soaked up their accolades and encouragement. Rehab and PT have been a true pain, but the regimen is definitely paying off. Dr. Smith began his questions and review of health issues and medicines. He talked briefly with Bob before he asked for my observations. I have been dispensing all meds since Bob began to have trouble keeping his schedule and dosages accurately. The office visit seemed to go well, and I thanked this physician who has played a key role in keeping Bob alive over the years.

On the drive home my husband said, "I do not want to go to Doctor Smith any more."

"Why is that?"

"Because he talks to you; he doesn't talk to me. It is like I do not exist. He treats me like I am inferior, because I can't think and do things like I used to."

"Bob, he cares about you, and we have to keep going to him. Besides, he gives us samples of your medicine, and, if we had to buy it, the cost would be $168 a month for just that one he gives us."

The silence lasted until dinnertime.

Things have changed. I hate the new reality Bob and I face. Because of his diseases, we are no longer equal. Doctor Smith made that quite clear.

Prayer: Gracious and Compassionate God, thank you for judging people with equity. Teach us all, doctors included, that sorting people into in-groups, out-groups, and subgroups is a foolish human pastime. May we simply love one another and leave the judgment up to you. Amen.

5

Jigsaw Puzzles

Scripture Reading: Luke 15:1-7

*And when he comes home, he calls together his friends and
neighbors, saying to them, "Rejoice with me, for I have found
my sheep that was lost."*

Luke 15:6

We know today's scripture as "The Parable of the Lost Sheep."
I believe that is a misnomer. A more appropriate title is "The
Parable of the Found Sheep," with emphasis on the finding by
the diligent shepherd who valued a silly sheep so much, only the
animal's safe return would suffice.

Previously, upon hearing this parable, I identified with the
wayward lamb. However, this morning I imagined myself as the
shepherd. I remembered my husband's close calls with death
when I thought he was "lost" forever. One of those times
occurred when he required surgery to remove three crushed vertebrae from his neck and to secure his head to his body with a
large titanium plate and screws.

The surgery was hazardous, tedious, and lasted eight hours.
The special operating table was designed to flip, so that after
Bob's neck was cut open and cleaned out from the front, he could
be turned over to be cut from the back, and then back to the front
again for closure. Then, for the third time, Bob was placed in a
gruesome halo screwed, literally, into the skull.

Recovery did not go well. Apparently, the surgery damaged

the muscles used for swallowing. Bob grew weaker and went from a regular room to ICU. I took up residence in a miserable, uncomfortable, noisy, waiting room for eleven days and ten nights. The doctors and nurses advised me not to go home (an hour away) but to remain nearby.

The experience is a blur—except for the jigsaw puzzles. Next to two large tables under the windows were stacks of puzzles in boxes. Hour after hour, day after day, night after night, I put together pieces to replicate the pictures on the box lids. I became a woman possessed and only left my post to spend ten minutes every hour on the hour with Bob, or to take care of basic needs. I became territorial, and, if people approached, I told them it was "my" puzzle on "my" table.

The curious thing about every one of those puzzles was that each had a missing piece. I hunted for the one thing that would make the picture complete, but I never found it. By the time Bob improved enough to be moved to a room, I had learned a valuable lesson. Like those jigsaw puzzles, I have a missing piece. Only God can fill the God-shaped hole in my soul.

Prayer: Good Shepherd, my heart is restless until it is filled with you. Thank you for finding me amongst the jigsaw puzzles. Amen.

6
Anxiety Attack

—◦◦◦◦◦—

Scripture Reading: 1 Peter 5:6-11

Cast all your anxiety on him, because he cares for you.

1 Peter 5:7

My husband sat in his recliner yelling my name. I could sense pain and panic in his voice. "Nell, I'm having one of those attacks. You know what it is. I can never remember what it's called. I can't stand this feeling. What's happening?"

When I rushed into the room, I saw the fear in his eyes and the twisting hands. I asked, "Are you having an anxiety attack? Is *anxiety* the word you can't remember?"

"Yes, it's awful. I'm losing control, and I don't know what to do."

Since I have had a few of these attacks on airplanes and in enclosed spaces, I know how horrible they are. Sitting next to his chair, I reached for his hand and encouraged him to do a few things that helped me get through similar experiences.

"Bob, I want you to close your eyes and lean back into your chair. Now, take some deep breaths. Slowly inhale the good air. Now slowly, very slowly, breathe out the bad, anxious air. I am going to say the Jesus Prayer as we breathe together. It goes like this. Breathe in: *Jesus Christ, Son of the Living God*. Breathe out: *Have mercy on me, a sinner*. We are going to repeat that again and again. Don't force. Let your breathing find an easy, natural rhythm. When all the bad air seems to be gone, change what you say when you exhale. Say, *You love me, and you take my anxiety away.*"

Bob closed his eyes and followed my instructions. He relaxed, and the episode passed. However, over the next few months, the attacks came more frequently. We asked the doctor about them. His solution was to switch Bob's antidepressant to a new drug known to be well suited to diabetics. The change was immediate; anxiety attacks are extremely rare now.

During those dark days we came to know that the God of all grace will restore, support, strengthen, and calm those who suffer. Now, when our hearts are overwhelmed, Bob and I are more aware of our need to cry to the Lord, to take refuge in God, and to rely on God. We take comfort in God's care.

———————————

Prayer: Thank you, dear Lord, for using our weaknesses to humble us, for that is how we are opened to the inflow of your grace. We grow when we stand in the transforming presence of your healing love. We praise you, and we adore you. Amen.

7

Anniversary Waltz

Scripture Reading: Hosea 11:1-11

I [God] led them with cords of human kindness,
with bands of love.
I was to them like those
who lift infants to their cheek.

Hosea 11:4

Today is our anniversary. We had some good years and made many happy memories before Bob got sick and then sicker. He has asked me several times, "Why don't you just bail out? Look what I've done to your life. This can't be any fun for you. You work so hard all the time taking care of me."

"Yes, Bob, my life is limited, but you need to understand I never entered this marriage for fun. I made my covenant out of love and the desire to grow a lasting relationship with you."

"Bless your heart, I don't know why you stick around, but I am thankful. I love you."

Two years ago my husband would not have been able to speak so eloquently. He was too ill and debilitated to feed or even "toilet" himself. Many care receivers are cognizant enough to appreciate those who provide for their needs. Like Bob, they see the physical and emotional costs for their care-givers and helplessly wish things could be different. I often wonder which is more difficult: being a recipient or being a giver. But I don't remember either of us having a choice. And given the chance to marry this blue-eyed Irishman, I'd do it all over again.

We won't celebrate with dining and dancing this year. My anniversary waltz will take place in my heart as I admire the altar flowers when we go to church today. I ordered the flowers in celebration of my years with Bob but also in thanksgiving for a God who never quits on me. God's love is everlasting regardless of debilitations of mind, body, or soul. Like a father, God stoops down, picks up his children, and holds them next to his cheek — so loving and intimate. Human beings are willful and silly and chase after other gods, but God fulfills God's part of the covenant relationship. *Always*.

Prayer: Yahweh, no matter how rebellious your people are, you never abandon them. As we caregivers spend whatever number of days we may have with our beloved, may we remember Love creates phenomenal dance partners. Amen.

8
A Broken Promise

───❧❧❧───

Scripture Reading: Hebrews 10:19-25

*Let us hold fast to the confession of our hope without
wavering, for [God] who has promised is faithful.*

Hebrews 10:23

In a classroom on the third floor of a large metropolitan church,
an amazing octogenarian facilitates a bimonthly support group
for persons with a family member who has Alzheimer's, dementia, or Parkinson's disease. During the meeting, Polly skillfully
asks each one about the status of the care receiver and also about
his or her own personal well-being.

Today, when Polly asked Glenda how she is doing, Glenda
turned to the young woman seated next to her. She patted her on
the shoulder and said, "I don't know what I would do without
Joyce. She brings me to these meetings and drives me everywhere I need to go. She's the best daughter-in-law anyone could
hope for." I thought about the Bible story of Ruth and Naomi.

Glenda paused. It was a long, pregnant pause, but Polly let it
continue uninterrupted until Glenda was ready to speak. The sobs
were barely audible, and then the words, between stifled crying,
spilled out. "I broke my promise. I promised my husband I would
never put him in a nursing home, and now I broke my promise."

The daughter-in-law reached for Glenda's hand. "But you had to."

"I didn't know what else to do. It was so awful; I can't forget
how scared I was. My husband yelled and screamed at me, and

he would not stop. Every time I went into the room where he was, he would start again at the top of his lungs threatening me. I can't even visit him in the nursing home because he reacts so horribly to me. We have been married fifty-three years this August, and it has all come down to this."

Most of us have heard Glenda tell her story before, in almost the exact same words. The tears still come. I especially relate to her because my husband pressured me into making the identical promise never to place him in a nursing home. I have agreed to keep him at home under hospice care when he approaches his "New Life."

Polly leaned forward and spoke to the woman stuck in her shock and grief. "Glenda, please don't feel guilty. Your husband is sick. He's not the man you married or even the man you made that promise to. Please remember to separate the person from the disease."

———

Prayer: Faithful and Loving God, be with Glenda and those people in similar dilemmas—people in the midst of pain, heartache, and disappointment. Help us remember the hope we have in you who keeps promises eternally. Amen.

9
His Eye Is on the Sparrow

—∞∞∞—

Scripture Reading: Matthew 10:29-31

So do not be afraid; you are of more value than many sparrows.

Matthew 10:31

With ambivalent feelings of sadness and relief, we sold our house with large yard, pool, and stairs, and moved into a small duplex. Gardening is a favorite pastime of mine. I hated leaving my little flora friends, bird and butterfly buddies, and ladybug brigade. But I comforted myself with the idea I could have flower beds, put up a bird feeder, and attract new pals to our new residence. I asked the landlord and received permission to start my "garden."

A lawn maintenance man removed overgrown bushes and helped establish composted flower beds. I transplanted a few bulbs and flower "starts" from the old yard. I set the trellis, bird-baths, big potted plants, and garden art throughout the new space. In two months, the landscape was flourishing.

The new bird feeder stands outside our dining room window. At our former residence, little black-capped chickadees, red cardinals, tufted titmice, and house wrens came to feed. Now, all we attract is a plentiful supply of twittering sparrows and mourning doves with their plaintive coo. I was disappointed in the lack of variety until one Sunday when the church choir sang "His Eye Is on the Sparrow." Because of that song, the small gluttonous sparrows at my feeder grow in importance and value every time we watch and listen to them during a meal.

As I listened deeply to the song's words that Sunday, I experienced a spiritual catharsis. Several times throughout the next week, I found myself softly singing the song:

> Why should I feel discouraged, why should the
>   shadows come,
> Why should my heart be lonely and long for
>   heaven and home,
> When Jesus is my portion? My constant friend
>   is He:
> His eye is on the sparrow, and I know He
>   watches me.

Was this song God's way of speaking to me? I believed it was. I learned, via the Internet, that Civilla Martin wrote the lyrics in 1905, following a visit to a bedridden friend and her crippled husband, the Doolittles. Mrs. Martin's husband asked the couple their secret for hopefulness and happiness despite their afflictions. Mrs. Doolittle's reply was simple: "His eye is on the sparrow, and I know He watches me." The next day Mrs. Martin mailed her poem to Charles Gabriel, who wrote the music.

Prayer: Thank you, dear God, for little sparrows. Thank you for the beautiful expression of boundless faith that inspired a song that reminds people of your constant love and provision no matter the circumstances. Amen.

10
Stuck

Scripture Reading: Psalm 69:1-18

*With your faithful help rescue me
from sinking in the mire.*

Psalm 69:13-14

Today I had a chance meeting in the public library. I talked with a friend from our old neighborhood who was gathering reading materials for her entire family to take on their long flight to Hawaii. The vacation is a twenty-fifth wedding anniversary present. They are a hardworking, faith-filled family who deserve this gift. I am glad for *their* trip, but I could not help the twinge of longing to have *my* own holiday.

I was still working as a children's librarian when we had our last vacation several years ago. We rented a house at the beach for the week following the completion of a highly demanding, successful summer reading program. A daughter and her family were able to get off and join us, and those surfside days massaged my soul. The sound of waves lapping the sandy shore, the harsh cries of gulls, and the salty breeze kissing my face tickled my deepest deep. I smiled and laughed and felt youthful.

Crystal Beach on Bolivar Peninsula lies east of Galveston Island and is reached by ferry. The sand is pale gold, not white. A strip of the beach has been packed down by vehicles crammed with young people cruising back and forth on weekends. I convinced a skeptical Bob I could drive the SUV beachside and unload his motorized wheelchair so he could "stroll" with the rest of us. When his chair got stuck in the sand, we laughed and raced to his rescue. He spent those first vacation days indoors alone doing crosswords, but later he allowed himself to be included in the beach scene. We even carried him down and placed him in the surf. We no longer felt guilty about leaving him, and the fun tripled for everyone.

But that was the last vacation. Since then we've made a few trips to visit my elderly mother and the grandchildren, but those are rare events becoming rarer. Bob is "stuck" at home in a mire of chronic pain and limited mobility. I invite him and try my best manipulative tactics to entice him out into the world. He goes to numerous doctor appointments and attends weekly church services and monthly Coin Club meetings, but otherwise he wants to stay home. I have trouble understanding his "stuck-ness," but my care receiver tells me, "It hurts too bad to go out."

Prayer: O God, when we are sinking in deep mire, we have hope, comfort, and the blessed assurance you will hear our cries and rescue us. For your steadfast love and unfailing mercy that accompany us everywhere we go or get stuck, we give you thanks and praise. Amen.

11
Up Against the Wall

—∞∞∞—

Scripture Reading: Jude 20-21

*Look forward to the mercy of our Lord Jesus Christ
that leads to eternal life.*

Jude 21

Lately my husband has had trouble breathing and swallowing. Bob has a metal plate in his neck, and he believes it has shifted, causing the latest difficulties. Bob and I trust our primary care doctor, and we had an appointment with him this morning. Another doctor had suggested we consult a neurosurgeon, so we wanted to know his take on that idea and if the recommended doctor was reputable. Dr. Jones reviewed Bob's medical history with us and concluded we could try the consultation. In his opinion, however, Bob is too high-risk to be a viable candidate for surgery.

Dr. Jones believes the surgeon will suggest a neck brace or collar instead. We've been through numerous attempts at fitting Bob with neck gear. He finds the braces and collars cause unbearable pain, and in a few months he stops wearing them. His past pattern of disliking external devices led me quickly to conclude a brace was not an option.

I sat in Dr. Jones's examination room with tears in my eyes thinking about what life is like at home. I watch Bob struggle to swallow his pills and his food. His breathing is often shallow and wheezy. He has oxygen equipment, but the windpipe seems constricted. My heart hurts from watching him suffer. I quietly commented, "It looks like there is nothing else we can do."

Dr. Jones shook our hands and told us to "hang in there."

Going home, Bob apologized for the trouble he causes. I responded, "Bob, I wish these trips to medical professionals could solve your awful dilemma. It looks like we are up against the wall, and no amount of pushing is going to get the damn thing to move. I don't know what we can do."

Bob replied, "We can pray."

He's right. Prayer does not have to provide solutions. The very act of praying brings comfort and solace. Bob and I both like an old hymn with these familiar words:

> Sweet hour of prayer! sweet hour of prayer! that
>   calls me from a world of care,
> and bids me at my Father's throne make all my
>   wants and wishes known.
> In seasons of distress and grief, my soul has often
>   found relief,
> and oft escaped the tempter's snare by thy return,
>   sweet hour of prayer!

Prayer: Savior God, we hasten to the place of prayer where you listen to our every care, and your faithfulness blesses our waiting souls. Amen.

12
Storms of the Heart

—◦◦◦◦—

Scripture Reading: Psalm 107:23-32

He made the storm be still,
and the waves of the sea were hushed.

Psalm 107:29

During a conversation with a young man at church, I learned he is excited about his job in youth ministry. He politely inquired about my work. I explained I am retired but hard at work on a daily devotional for caregivers.

"My grandmother sure needs that. Let me know when I can buy it for her."

"Oh, your grandmother is a caregiver? For your grandfather? What are his health issues, if you don't mind my asking?"

After he briefed me on the situation, I commented, "I sure do understand what your grandmother faces. It's so difficult to be a healthy spouse. Most of us have to deal with a lot of anger."

"Oh, you nailed it. She's angry. Last week she offered me her frequent flyer miles and said she knew she would never be able to travel again. She's also sad and lonely."

"Yes, many caregivers have an overwhelming sense of isolation, which compounds the anger. An occasional phone call from a thoughtful grandson can help."

Phone calls and cards from relatives and friends encourage us. Caregiving tosses us into a bewildering spiritual journey not of our own choosing. I have discovered storms of anger can build in our hearts and mess with our souls. With each new sandbar and roiling wave, the anger surfaces, and we have to fumble for a life vest one more time. Our care receivers are in pain, depressed, coping with the latest problems, but so are we.

People have different ways of dealing with caregiving maelstroms. One man (his wife had Alzheimer's) sometimes went into his garage and threw things at the wall. Crying spells provide great release and relief. Some people garden, work on the computer, keep a journal, or read. Some stomp around the dining room table in a rage. People try a variety of coping strategies — not always helpful. Aching hearts don't disappear with overindulgence in food, alcohol, or tranquilizers.

The most effective coping mechanism for me is a morning regimen of Bible study, daily devotions, and prayer. Anger is a major problem for me, and I have learned I can't do anger management by myself. I saw a framed saying that precisely describes what happens during my morning ritual: "Sometimes God calms the storm. . . . Sometimes He lets the storm rage and calms His child."

The psalmist reminds us God delivers those who cry to God in their trouble, and brings them out of their distress. God does not remove the problems but stills the inner storm and hushes the rolling sea.

Prayer: Great God, thank you for using our anger to draw us to fuller awareness of your presence. I pray this old sailor's prayer for your people: May they have "fair winds, following seas, and fond haven." Amen.

13
Amaryllis

— ∞∞ —

Scripture Reading: Isaiah 35:1-2, 10

*They shall obtain joy and gladness,
and sorrow and sighing shall flee away.*

Isaiah 35:10

The cold, gray winter days were getting me down. I lost my younger brother unexpectedly in early January. Then a lovely member of my Bible class died suddenly with pneumonia. Another member of the class went through the short illness and death of her husband. I was grieving and adrift in my confusion. The ice on the birdbath matched the chill in my spirit. I felt like a captive, exiled far from home. I knew this sad time would pass, but I was stuck and simply going through the motions of living while caring for my husband.

One day I decided to sort and put away the Christmas cards and gifts. I like to have things in their place, and it was unusual for a large pile to sit for weeks unattended. In one of the larger gift bags I found a metal box. Potting soil and a large amaryllis bulb were nestled inside the silvery box. I planted the bulb as instructed, watered the dirt, and set the container in the dining room window.

I faithfully kept the soil moist, but nothing happened. For four weeks I observed no change. Patience and the waiting for the blessing were rewarded when a little green shoot appeared. The plant grew so fast that every mealtime we noticed something new emerging. First, a stalk grew two feet up toward heaven. The bud on top began to show color, and, in a matter of days, three deep red, trumpet-like blooms heralded beauty and joy. My husband and I sat at the table and marveled at how God could put so much glory in one small bulb. A second stem appeared with two more blossoms to amaze us.

We have several isolated seniors and homebound caregivers on our Christmas gift list. It is a no-brainer what to give them next year—an amaryllis to cheer their spirits.

Prayer: O great Creator of us all, we marvel at how you can put so much beauty and life into one brown, dormant bulb. Thank you for a blessing of renewed hope found in patiently waiting for red flowers that penetrate grayness and "stuckness" of winter days. Amen.

Fences

Scripture Reading: Ephesians 2:13-18

*For he [Jesus] is our peace; in his flesh he has made both
groups into one and has broken down the dividing wall, that
is, the hostility between us.*

Ephesians 2:14

While preparing to lead a Bible study on Ephesians, I discovered a little story in a commentary by William Barclay. The story by Rita Snowden (1907–1999) is set in France during World War I. Briefly, it goes like this:

> Some soldiers took the body of a fallen comrade to a French cemetery for burial. The priest told them he first must ask if the dead man was baptized in the Roman Catholic Church. They said they did not know. The priest told the men he was very sorry, but in that case he could not permit burial in his churchyard. Sadly the soldiers took their comrade and buried him just outside the cemetery fence.
>
> The next day they came back to say prayers and pay tribute to the deceased, and to their astonishment they could not find the grave. Search as they might, they found no trace of freshly dug soil. As the bewildered men turned to leave, the priest ran up to them. He told them his heart was troubled because of his refusal to allow their dead comrade to be buried in the churchyard. So, early in the morning, he

rose from his bed and, with his own hands, moved the fence to include the body of the soldier who died for France.

Love can motivate wondrous and powerful acts like this one. Rules and regulations erected the fence; love moved it. The author of Ephesians (probably Paul) expressed gratitude and astonishment at what God accomplished through Christ Jesus. Jesus removed fences between people—Gentile and Jew, slave and free, male and female, old and young, healthy and sick, clean and unclean—because he revealed the flaws of religion founded solely on rules and laws. He invited humankind to religion founded in LOVE.

———————

Prayer: Great and Gracious God, teach us the ways of love in all our actions and words so that we may grow in our capacity to keep fences out of our relationships—especially the one with our care receiver that challenges us hourly day after day. Amen.

15
Overdose

———

Scripture Reading: Ecclesiastes 7:8-14

In the day of prosperity be joyful, and in the day of adversity consider; God has made the one as well as the other.

Ecclesiastes 7:14

Last night my husband sat in his recliner with his med tray on his lap. I was in the kitchen serving up dinner plates when I heard him say, "I think I put too much insulin in my shot. You told me four units, but I took forty. Sorry."

I've learned enough about diabetes to know this was a serious situation. Thanks to the advice of a diabetic friend in our Sunday school class, I keep a container of glucose tabs in my purse and in the kitchen for those times when the blood sugar gets too low. I grabbed two large tabs and told Bob to chew them while I reached for the phone to call our son, a family practice doctor.

"Get Dad to the hospital immediately. Which one is the closest? I'll call and tell them to expect you. He has about thirty minutes before he could bottom out, so go now."

With the emergency lights flashing, I drove fast to the ER. En route, Bob talked about his cremation. He was feeling dizzy and somewhat confused by the time we pulled up to the hospital entrance. He had been doing so well for weeks; I was in disbelief he could be close to dying. The ER team responded quickly, and nine hours later we were back home as if we had not been to the edge one more time.

This was a wake-up call to imminent danger. Bob had overdosed on insulin, but I had almost overdosed on illusion—the illusion that Bob had totally regained his mental acuity and I could ease up in my watchdog role. I knew he could not do math and number functions correctly, but I wanted so badly for him to be his old self, I failed to see reality. He functions okay in many ways, but not in others. No matter how deeply I wish it were so, he never will be the old Bob. I need to let go of unrealistic fantasies as I push toward the truth. I must now take control of the insulin as well as the pills.

Many caregivers interpret the "good times" and lucid moments as signs that our loved ones are coming back. The Teacher in Ecclesiastes reminds us simply to enjoy what we have now while avoiding the trap of wishful longing for former days.

———————

Prayer: Loving God, close calls get our attention. Thank you for allowing us to greet a new day together. Teach each of us care providers how to be a wise helpmate for our loved one. Amen.

16
Blessed Assurance

———∞∞∞———

Scripture Reading: Hebrews 6:9-12

*And we want each one of you to show the same diligence so as
to realize the full assurance of hope to the very end.*

Hebrews 6:11

A woman I strongly admire phoned this afternoon to thank me
for an encouragement card I had sent. Janet cared for her spouse
for more than twenty years after he became paraplegic in an accident. Before Frank died this spring, their son, in his forties, was
diagnosed with bone cancer in addition to other serious health
problems. A petite woman who carries a heavy burden, Janet is
a remarkable example of a dear soul strengthened and sustained
by faith. No doubt she has her messy days like the rest of us, yet
she walks with "the full assurance of hope" mentioned in today's
scripture.

Janet's serene approach to her life reminds me of an old hymn.
"Blessed Assurance" is one of about eight thousand texts written
by nineteenth-century gospel hymn writer Fanny Crosby. The
lyrics express the author's childlike trust in a caring God who
watches over her.

Fanny was born in Putnam County, New York, in 1820. She
lost her sight at the age of six weeks when a poultice was applied
improperly to her eyes. At age fifteen she entered the Institution
of the Blind in New York City, remaining there for twenty-three
years, first as a student and then as a teacher. In 1858 she mar-

ried Alexander Van Alstyne, a teacher in the same school, who was blind like her. They had one child, a daughter who died in infancy.

By age eight, Fanny's gift for writing poetry was apparent to her family and teachers. She was often asked to write and read for special events, including an appearance before Congress on behalf of the blind. Poems and lyrics for both secular songs and hymns poured from this gifted woman of faith. She left teaching to do mission work among the poor—work that often inspired her writing. Fanny's husband died in 1902, and she died in 1915 at the age of ninety-four.

Fanny wrote "Sunday School Hymns," warmhearted songs with simple, pleasing melodies that awakened a popular enthusiasm felt to this day in both America and England. When I learned the author of "Blessed Assurance" was a blind woman, the words of the second verse swelled with poignancy:

> Perfect submission, perfect delight,
>   visions of rapture now burst on my sight;
> angels descending bring from above
>   echoes of mercy, whispers of love.

Prayer: Gracious God, we are grateful for those you send to enrich our lives with profound faith in adverse circumstances. Grant us this day the blessed assurance of hope they have found in Jesus. Amen.

17
Looking for a Cure

─◆◆◆◆─

Scripture Reading: Lamentations 3:19-26

The thought of my affliction and my homelessness
is wormwood and gall!
My soul continually thinks of it
and is bowed down within me.

Lamentations 3:19-20

My husband sat at the table with head bowed and eyes closed. Often when he assumes this posture he is praying, but many times it is just the way he sits. He had eaten most of his lunch when he spoke. "I'm afraid I'm getting depressed."

"Bob, tell me what makes you think that."

"I can't carry this heavy burden much longer. I am tired and I hurt so bad. You know that woman on TV who talks about a cure for the disease I have—what's the disease I have? You know the woman I mean."

"Are you trying to remember *diabetes*? And is the woman Mary Tyler Moore?"

"Yes. Well, she talks about finding a cure for diabetes, but it's not going to happen. I hate this disease. It is hard to live while you're dying. They aren't going to find a cure for any of the stuff I have while I'm still alive."

"Bob, researchers are working hard and have made phenomenal strides."

"Won't happen in the next twenty years."

I grabbed this opportunity to be silent for a change. It was no time to discuss the difference between healing and cure. Bob wouldn't understand that curing is what doctors do when they eliminate the disease, while healing is what patients do in a deeply personal inner process as they return to wholeness. The inner work is done by the physical body but also involves a process of the soul that elicits a desire for life itself. Bob won't be cured, but he can find healing.

As I sipped the last of my iced tea, I realized my anxious feelings came from a perpetual desire to say something comforting and wise, to ease Bob's mental and physical anguish, to make the hideous, interminable suffering disappear. Then it occurred to me Bob's depression may have a beneficial flip side. His deep mood may indicate a necessary stage in his life journey that leads toward integration and acceptance of his situation.

Thomas Moore, in *Care of the Soul: A Guide for Cultivating Depth and Sacredness in Everyday Life*, says depression is a rite of passage to higher levels of self-realization. Bob's depression may have its own angel leading him to special insights. His "halo of melancholy" may be indicative of a cathartic emptiness leading him toward the "peace that passes understanding." Time to let go of my need to fix and to let God and Bob work this one out.

———————

Prayer: Great is your faithfulness, O God, our Savior. You did not rescue Jesus from his dark night of self-emptying love, but you had a greater plan. May we care providers trust you have a plan for our loved ones too. Amen.

18
He Touched Me

———

Scripture Reading: Mark 8:22-25

*Then Jesus laid his hands on his eyes again; and he looked
intently and his sight was restored, and he saw
everything clearly.*

Mark 8:25

In a small French country village during World War II there
stood a marble figure of Jesus with hands outstretched. The
statue graced the courtyard of a quaint little church. One day a
bomb struck so close that the statue was dismembered.

When the battle was over and the enemy had passed through,
citizens of the village decided to find the pieces of their beloved
statue and reconstruct it. They gathered the broken pieces and
reassembled the statue. To them, the scars on the body added to
the sculpture's beauty. But there was one problem: they were
unable to find the hands.

"A Christ without hands is no Christ at all," someone lamented.
"Hands with scars, yes. But what is a Lord without hands? We
need a new statue."

Another person came along with a different idea. This one pre-
vailed. Today a brass plaque attached to the base of the statue
reads: "I have no hands but your hands."

I read this story years ago, and it came to mind today as I
recalled conversations this week with three different caregivers.
One woman who lives with her aged, ailing mother shared with

me how difficult it is to keep the house clean, especially now that her mom is suffering from digestive ailments. A man related his experience of going to visit his frail mother and finding feces all over the rug and bathroom. A third person told me about the long, painful hours holding her husband's hand as he lay dying from Parkinson's disease.

Caregivers do hard, difficult work. Their hands scrub, disinfect, wash, cook, launder, bathe, fasten buttons and zippers, wipe, and, in some cases, diaper. They also hug, hold, pat, touch, and massage their care receivers. Those hands are often folded or outstretched in humble petition: *Come, Lord Jesus, enter this place and provide strength—the superhuman kind of strength required to get me through the day.*

In our scripture story today, Jesus healed a blind man when the man begged Jesus to touch him. Everywhere I allow Jesus to touch my life, something happens. I want to be the hands, feet, breath, and heart of Jesus not out of duty but out of love. More often than not, I begrudge cleaning the bathroom and wiping up spills, but when I remember my hands are Jesus' hands, it softens my hardened heart.

Prayer: Jesus Christ, touch us anew each morning. Stir within us a joy in being your servant today, even if the challenges are terribly difficult and unpleasant. Amen.

19
Missing Person

Scripture Reading: Ezekiel 34:11-16

I will seek the lost, and I will bring back the strayed, and I will bind up the injured, and I will strengthen the weak.

Ezekiel 34:16

After dismissing the morning Bible class, I dashed across town to pick up my husband, Bob. For two weeks I had been asking if he wanted to see the dentist about a mouth ulcer, but every day he responded, "It will get better." Today while I scrambled to get my discussion questions ready for class, he announced, "Nell, my mouth feels worse. I need to see a dentist. NOW!"

The only available appointment was during class time, but it was close enough to the end of class that I could pick Bob up. I made arrangements for a cab to take him, wrote down phone numbers on a piece of paper, set out a clean shirt and jeans — organized everything. Then I left for my study group.

When I arrived later at the dentist's office, the receptionist informed me Bob had never showed. I scurried home. He was not there. A phone call to the cab company informed me a driver picked him up on time, but because of invasion of privacy rules, the dispatcher could not tell me where the taxi took him.

I filed a missing person report. The police could obtain facts from Yellow Cab. It seemed strange describing the physical characteristics of my husband and then waiting. I felt like a trapeze artist who has let go of one swing and waits in midair to catch the other swing—not out of control but certainly in limbo. Not flying through the air with the greatest of ease, I prayed and tried to calm my breathing.

Three hours after Bob went missing, the phone rang. He was at a restaurant in a town twenty-five miles away. He had lost the information card I told him to keep in his wallet. When Bob went into a store to find a phone directory for our number, the cabbie, who "had other things to do beside drive him around all day," took off without being paid. Apparently the driver, recently arrived in the U.S. from Algeria, had argued with the confused, lost, elderly man. Some kind soul helped Bob make the call and gave him a free Coke.

On the way home, Bob told me, "I am not going to apologize to anyone, because I don't have anything to apologize for. I just can't remember names and places and phone numbers and directions anymore."

It is time to order one of those "safe return" bracelets.

Prayer: O Lord God, you are a vigilant God who seeks and finds your wandering sheep when they are lost. We caregivers can trust your compassion and concern for our loved ones. Amen.

20
Lame Horse, Rotten Wood

~∞∞~

Scripture Reading: 2 Corinthians 12:7b-10

I am content with weaknesses, insults, hardships, persecutions, and calamities for the sake of Christ; for whenever I am weak, then I am strong.

2 Corinthians 12:10

My best friend, Emily, travels extensively and often brings me an unusual gift from a trip. I keep one of those gifts on my desk next to the computer keyboard, handy to see or touch for inspiration.

The object of my affection and encouragement is an elongated wooden cross two-by-seven inches. The front surface is rough, irregular, deeply cracked, and gouged. The back is smooth and sanded. The crude front gives the cross profound natural character. The limb from which it was carved obviously had seen many seasons of stress.

A small card enclosed with the cross identified the artist, Margaret Bailey. I tracked down information about her, via the Internet, by way of the quotation on the card. Not long after Margaret made her first cross she found these words often attributed to fourteenth-century mystic Julian of Norwich:

> God rides the lame horse,
> God carves the rotten wood.

The quote resonates with Margaret because she finds inspiration for her crosses by studying the split, partially rotten or weathered wood she uses. The eye of the artist combined with the eye of faith understands Julian the mystic meant human beings are wood that is rotten, weathered, or broken (and the horse that is lame). Yet God not only finds a use for us but also transforms us into the divine imageless image. Margaret never rejects a flawed piece of wood. On a spiritual level, God never rejects a flawed human being. Often it's true that the greater the flaw, the more astounding the transformation.

Some years ago, soon after a narrow escape from death, Margaret was driving down Main Street in Houston near Rice University when she felt compelled to go into a church. She believed God wanted something from her. She prayed for discernment and soon discovered her calling. With pieces of rough native Texas woods (cedar, pecan, mesquite, and driftwood), a small fretsaw, a rasp, and some sandpaper, she began to make crosses. They now reside in offices, homes, and sanctuaries all over the world.

Through the Cross, Jesus took upon himself the ultimate mark of human nature—the mark of death. He assumed the worst life can do. He experienced the depths of hurt and grief to which the human heart can sink. God examines the human soul and sees the weathering, the rot, the brittleness, and the limp. In spite of it all, God finds beauty and strength in each one.

———————

Prayer: Gracious Lord, we feel inadequate as caregivers. Nevertheless you redeem us from the scrap heap. Our hearts bubble over with gratitude. Amen.

21
Poker Games

Scripture Reading: Psalm 71:17-21

So even to old age and gray hairs,
O God, do not forsake me,
until I proclaim your might
to all the generations to come.

Psalm 71:18

Both my husband and I come from families that enjoy gathering every few weeks as well as on major holidays. Bountiful quantities of delicious food play a key role in these conclaves. There is, however, a difference in our family backgrounds when it comes to what happens after everyone has eaten to the point of discomfort. Bob's family plays poker. My family perpetuates the deep Southern tradition of sitting around (in rocking chairs, porch swings, etc.) talking. The subjects are wide-ranging. Often conversation includes stories about people—themselves, one another, someone who knows someone. Invariably there will be humor woven into the easy banter followed by spontaneous belly laughs. I have witnessed generations holding their stomachs while mirthful tears streamed down their cheeks.

One Sunday after church I hosted a family dinner for Bob. He has enjoyed these meals and card games with his relatives since he was a young lad. When I host a gathering at our home, Bob appreciates it even more because it is harder all the time for him to get out. He likes to have everyone stand in a circle holding hands while he says grace before we serve our plates. His faith is evident.

This was an especially meaningful gathering, because we had not seen some of the relatives in two months due to vacations, weddings, and other assorted activities. Also, it was the first time our granddaughter brought her serious beau to a family event. He fit right in.

Another reason the time proved special was the opportunity it provided to educate the family about what is going on with Bob without ever saying a word. Caregivers get weary of recounting their daily routine with its challenges and lonely isolation. Talk seems almost disrespectful of our care receiver.

The poker game turned into a perfect vehicle for the family to recognize the decline in Bob's mental acuity. I was in the living room with another nonplayer, but afterward I heard what happened. Bob said, "They helped me play cards. When I didn't put the right amount in the pot, Ellen [granddaughter] showed me what to put in. I didn't even know when I won, but Ella [niece] told me. Billy [nephew] shuffled the cards and dealt for me. Everybody helped me, and I think I won fifty cents. This has been a great day."

———————

Prayer: Heavenly Comforter, thank you for opportunities to share a feast of food, family, and love. Thank you too for helping loved ones discover dignified ways to deal with limitations and to realize the challenges we caregivers face daily. Show our families new ways to assist us with the cards we have been dealt. Amen.

22
Driver Dilemma

Scripture Reading: Psalm 15

O LORD, who may abide in your tent?
Who may dwell on your holy hill?
Those who walk blamelessly,
and do what is right.

Psalm 15:1-2

Many of the stories told at Alzheimer's/dementia/Parkinson's support group meetings are dramatic and memorable. Sometimes they're hilarious, sometimes heartbreaking. Most people are shy at first, but they soon learn about the strict confidentiality rule and that it isn't how a person says something that counts. Trusting enough to say anything is the first step to being incorporated in the group. True sharing is a venture into vulnerability, but our real self must come out so it can be healed and loved. Caregivers need healing and love like our care receivers do.

At a recent meeting, a new attendee, Cora, told about her husband in early-stage Alzheimer's. A seasoned group member asked whether he was still driving. Driving is a hot topic and major issue with chronically ill, impaired, and disabled persons—especially those in denial about their condition (perhaps the majority).

Cora said the physician had completed forms stating her husband has impaired ability to operate a motor vehicle and should no longer be allowed to drive. He signed the papers and gave them to Cora. Sneaky husband Pete went behind her back, renewed his license, and continues to drive to his office several days a week. She felt upset about being unable to convince Pete to stop. "He could hit someone, and he doesn't seem to understand he's flirting with danger. He simply won't listen."

A group member suggested she make copies of the doctor's restriction papers and send them with a letter to the state Department of Motor Vehicles. The license would be revoked, and Pete would never need to know she was involved in its revocation. There's a potential problem if Pete continues to drive, but at least Cora will have taken positive steps to encourage him to make our streets safer.

Driving has been a sticky dilemma for us too. Bob did not believe either me or the doctor when we said he should stop driving. Eventually I turned to the daughter who can talk with her dad as no one else can. Jill and her husband came over, and we did a kind of family intervention. We cited a recent noninjury accident Bob had had and continued to build our case, until Bob promised he would not get behind the wheel again.

To this day this stubborn Irishman believes he can still drive. Our daughter and I are stubborn too. He's lost his independence and it hurts. But he *is* doing what is right.

Prayer: Jesus, please help Pete and others like him to be wise. If we had all lived in Palestine with you, we would not have this issue—no motor vehicles. Amen.

23
Jimmy's Prayer

⁓⁓⁓

Scripture Reading: Matthew 6:7-13

*When you are praying, do not heap up empty phrases as the
Gentiles do; for they think that they will be heard
because of their many words.*

Matthew 6:7

Many caregivers are turned off by prayer. Perhaps it is because
of disinterest or frustration from not receiving the answers they
want. Others find prayer an important part of their lives, a way
of life that sustains them. Prayerful people are *real* down-to-earth
folks, very much human. Their piety is not pompous or phony or
condescending. Through the years I have learned there is no single method of prayer and no one way to encounter God. Prayer
is mysterious and personal—unique to the pray-er and the situation—even in formal liturgical settings.

One of my favorite stories about prayer comes from *Opening to
God* by Thomas Green.

> Jimmy [the laborer] was a simple man, of little formal edu-
> cation. Each day, when returning from work, he stopped in
> the church and sat in the back for several minutes. The
> parish priest noticed the regularity of Jimmy's visits, and his
> fervor. He wondered just what a simple man like Jimmy did
> during these visits. One day he asked him what happened.
> Jimmy replied: "Nothing much, Father. I just say, 'Jesus, it's

Jimmy.' And he says, 'Jimmy, it's Jesus.' And we're happy to be together."

For all my reading and theologizing about prayer, I often return to the simple truth I find in Jimmy's spontaneous yet honest prayer experience. If Jimmy finds the Lord this way, then his way is the right way for him. Jimmy's relationship to God is very deep, and nothing should be done to complicate it.

Listening is a great metaphor for prayer. The good pray-er is a good listener. Jimmy's prayer is a perfect example of dialogue when what was said depended upon what the other person said. This is not an example of two monologues running concurrently, but is instead a personal encounter in love.

Jimmy's story may be misleading in its simplicity. I tell it not to make him out to be a saint. We don't know his personal history. But I tell it to move all of us to a desire for the rare, real, simple, experiential faith of a person who has lived life with his eyes and ears open to an encounter with God. My prayer life too often begins from a posture of preoccupied self-centeredness. Yet I am desirous of something better, the Something More my soul longs to find. Today I need to pray like Jimmy.

———————

Prayer: Hello, Jesus; it's *(your name)*. I can hear you say, "*(Your name)*, it's Jesus." Help each one of us to take time daily to listen silently until we hear you call us by name and can feel your comforting Presence. Amen.

24
Roses

Scripture Reading: Psalm 51:10-12

*Restore to me the joy of your salvation,
and sustain in me a willing spirit.*

Psalm 51:12

William came in soon after the support group meeting began and took a seat at the corner of the table near me. He sat quietly listening as stories and remarks were shared. The facilitator turned to him and asked how he was doing. William praised home health for the tremendous aid they provide four days a week. The aides bathe his wife and tend to her grooming. They even feed her, so he can be freed up for a few hours to take care of business. On the other three days he is responsible for Jackie's care, which he finds difficult. He worries about what will happen when coverage for home health care runs out in a couple of months.

One of William's friends in the group said, "Tell them about your project." William held up a pack of note cards featuring a charcoal drawing of a large rose blossom. The shading and detail of the artwork were delicate and intricate. William explained he had assembled packets of ten "rose" cards to sell for five dollars with all proceeds going to the Alzheimer's Association. William turned to the back of a card and pointed to an inscription indicating his project is dedicated to his wife.

When asked about the artwork, he told about learning to draw with the help of one of the home health aides who is an artist. His wife has always loved roses, and he draws blooms inspired by the rose garden he maintains.

Someone asked William whether he continues to teach piano lessons at home, and he replied that he has given up all but his two oldest students, a man in his seventies and a woman who is fifty-five. He said it is not a formal arrangement, but the woman always puts a little money on the piano before she leaves.

William is dealing with his wife's late-stage Alzheimer's, yet he is still participating in a full life. He grows roses and has learned to draw from a teacher who happened to enter his home as a nurse's aide for his wife. And now he has come up with an inspired plan to reach beyond himself by contributing to an organization that makes a huge difference in millions of lives.

Life has dealt William a lousy hand, but he is winning the game. The rose symbolizes the emotion love. No wonder roses play such a significant role in this admirable man's life.

———————————

Prayer: Great Artist, thank you for your handiwork that blesses and refreshes our awe and wonder. Thank you for your servant who has found ways to renew his spirit and mind in the midst of his caregiving duties. Little things grow in loveliness, ever new, with you and William. Amen.

25
Take a Deep Breath

—∞∞∞—

Scripture Reading: Genesis 2:4b-9

*Then the Lord God formed man from the dust of the ground,
and breathed into his nostrils the breath of life;
and the man became a living being.*

Genesis 2:7

My husband did not wear his hearing aids to a pulmonary test at the hospital. The woman administering the test barked instructions like a drill sergeant at boot camp. Unlike a drill sergeant, though, she managed to be kind and courteous while barking, and she got great test results. She informed me Bob took the test three times with consistent results, which meant the pulmonary doctor would receive accurate data. I added Julie to a long list of skillful medical professionals who respect their patients. I thank God for them.

The steady drone of the oxygen machine has returned. Julie gave Bob some neat spongy cushions to fit around the tubing that goes over his ears and told him to use his oxygen pump 24/7. He does not like the restriction of wearing the nosepiece or being tethered to a machine and therefore had become a lapsed user. But his breathing problems have resurfaced with a vengeance, and back home it's my turn to bark about using the machine.

I have noticed Bob often thanks God in his prayers for "the very air we breathe." Nothing causes more panic and anxiety than not being able to get enough air into your body. Because I had asthma as a child and occasionally have episodes now, I feel tremendous empathy when Bob wheezes and gasps for air.

This morning the sound of the oxygen machine triggered a reflection on the Hebrew word *ruach*, which means breath, wind, spirit. The scriptures are full of this word with its layers of rich and intriguing applications. In the second Creation story God breathes the breath of life into a lump of dirt to make a living creature. The breath permeates the whole being, extends the principle of life, and imparts divine creative energy. Powerful words from the book of Job express this concept well. Elihu speaks, "The Spirit of God has made me, and the breath of the Almighty gives me life"(Job 33:4).

At the time of Jesus' baptism, "the Spirit of God descend[ed] like a dove and alight[ed] on him" (Matt. 3:16). The first time Jesus stood to read in the synagogue, he read from the scroll of Isaiah: "The Spirit of the Lord is upon me" (Luke 4:18). As the Gospel story unfolds, the Spirit of Jesus comes to represent the presence and activity of God as well as the continuing presence of Jesus in his disciples through the gift of the Holy Spirit.

Prayer: Spirit of the Living God, fall afresh on your people. Spirit of Jesus Christ, fill us with deep gulps of your life-giving love. Amen.

26
The Right Time

———

Scripture Reading: Ecclesiastes 3:1-8

There is a time for everything,
and a season for every activity under heaven.

Ecclesiastes 3:1, NIV

"Please, someone, tell me how you know when it is the right time to put your spouse in a nursing home."

Myra begged the Alzheimer's/dementia/Parkinson's support group for help with what she called "the toughest point in my life." Her voice grew louder and her hands more animated as she talked. Her husband has Alzheimer's, Parkinson's, and serious heart problems. She told us each condition presents a difficult challenge, but to deal with three problems has made her life "unbearable." Medicine for the Alzheimer's makes the Parkinson's worse and vice versa. The man is a powder keg waiting for a match. His caregiver is a powder keg too.

The community of experienced caregivers at the meeting shared some profound and compassionate words. Polly, the facilitator, said, "How to know the right time for putting your spouse in a care facility is hard. I remember when I was pregnant with my first child, I asked the obstetrician how I would know it was time to go to the hospital. He told me, 'You will know.' And I did."

Polly continued, "Forgive me if I sound flip. I don't mean to at all. Let me pass along something that helped me when Steve became so sick. The counselor at the Alzheimer's Association office explained there are two parties involved in determining the right time: the care receiver *and* the caregiver. The factors to weigh are when the patient reaches the point he or she needs more skilled care than the caregiver can provide and/or when the caregiver is worn out and on the verge of becoming ill from the responsibility."

Linda joined the conversation. "Many people asked why I didn't put my husband in a nursing home. Several of you know how it feels to want to hang on. I probably waited too long, but once I made the decision (against my son's wishes, I might add), the move went well. The staff takes good care of him there. I wish I had moved him sooner. I visit almost every day, even though Dan doesn't know me. I talk to him and I take magazines. He doesn't understand what he is looking at, but he enjoys turning the pages. Plus I discovered he loves Wendy's Frosties, and he smiles when he sees me coming with one."

Myra informed us her husband is difficult, and she thinks she cannot handle one more minute. The next day when he is loving and easy to control, she vacillates.

The scripture reminds us there is "a season for every activity under heaven."

Prayer: Lord of all our years, be present with Myra and others facing tough decisions about the care of their loved ones. May we never forget it is always the right time to be with you in prayer. Amen.

27
The Lamp

Scripture Reading: Matthew 5:14-16

No one after lighting a lamp puts it under the bushel basket,
but on the lampstand, and it gives light to all in the house.

Matthew 5:15

Teaching Bible classes to fifteen or more women on Wednesday mornings presents immense challenge and gratification. I have had the opportunity to study with some remarkable Bible scholars. I enjoy sharing insights and helping students make connections between scripture and their life journeys.

Sessions begin when I light a candle and say, "Thy word is a lamp unto my feet, and a light unto my path" (Ps. 119:105, KJV). They conclude with prayer requests from the class. Over the past two years one member has requested prayers for her husband. His failing eyesight and inability to drive are only the latest problems. "Welcome, Susan, to my world." We laughed with relief. We knew we would be companions for one another during our unpredictable futures.

One morning the doorbell rang. Susan, who serves as administrator for the class, entered with their end-of-the-year gift for the teacher. The intricate Celtic cross and lovely chain purchased from a gifted local silversmith are exquisite. We chatted a bit. I told her about a lamp I found for my husband, and the immense difference it is making for him. The swing-arm adjustable lamp features a magnifying glass and light attached to the end. Bob can

66

now see fine print and examine coins from his massive collection. Susan left knowing the cost and where she might purchase one. The next day an e-mail of thanks informed me Susan's husband was overjoyed to receive the new lamp. This simple piece of equipment is changing the quality of his life, as it did Bob's.

I am surprised by the number of opportunities to share care-giver experiences and hard-earned "wisdoms." From my support group and interaction with other caregivers I know people are eager to help one another. They do not hide their lamp under a bushel but offer it up to light the difficult, stony, uncertain paths of others. Their gifts are humble and seemingly insignificant to some-one who has never "walked the walk." There is no self-aggrandize-ment in any form. Their servant job is a powerful equalizer opening them to hospitality toward everyone. I think we might add a beatitude to the Sermon on the Mount: Blessed are the care-givers, for they reflect the Lamplight of God's love and generosity.

Prayer: Shine in our hearts, Lord Jesus, so we may be more and more like you, the Light of the world. And to God be the glory now and forever. Amen.

28
Stitched Prayer

—❧—

Scripture Reading: Luke 11:9-13

*So I say to you, Ask, and it will be given you; search, and
you will find; knock, and the door will be opened for you.*

Luke 11:9

On the wall next to my computer desk hangs a framed needlework rendition of the Serenity Prayer. Thirty years have passed
since I spotted the kit at The Stitchery. A garland of flowers,
intertwining leafy vines, and small butterflies surround and
emphasize the loveliness of the prayer words.

> God, grant me the serenity to accept the things I
>   cannot change,
> Courage to change those things I can,
> And wisdom to know the difference.

When I stitched the prayer, I had no idea it was a credo in
twelve-step programs, but I knew I longed, craved, desired with
all my heart to have serenity, courage, and wisdom. Nothing has
changed.

The prayer was included in a sermon by American theologian,
author, minister, and teacher Reinhold Niebuhr (1892–1971),
probably around 1940. An expanded version of the prayer, ori-
gins unknown, continues with these additional lines:

> Living one day at a time;
> Enjoying one moment at a time;

Accepting hardships as the pathway to peace;
Taking, as [Christ] did, this sinful world
As it is, not as I would have it;
Trusting that [God] will make all things right
If I surrender to [God's] will;
So that I may be reasonably happy in this life
And supremely happy with [God]
Forever and ever in the next.

I find myself crying out to God anew these days. Bob's loss of memory and growing list of health issues leave me reeling. Sometimes my soul seems to be in turmoil, and life seems so damned difficult I want to scream. At times I dream of running away from my troubles. Occasionally I am able to take action to change the situations troubling me, but more often than not I am powerless to do anything more than pray. In those times I find comfort in the Serenity Prayer.

When all seems to be going okay, bam! Here comes something new to challenge us. We were jolted this week by Bob's dental problems and his getting lost for three hours. Unpredictability characterizes caregiving more than anything, and that has me begging God to grant what I need to get through one more day. I have serious doubts I'll ever receive serenity, but I knock and hope it will be behind the next door.

Prayer: Ever-patient Listener, caregivers feel so helpless and powerless. Incline your ear to our prayers, for we are troubled. You promise to give to those who ask, and we ask for a simple and serene life. Help us to accept joyfully our care ministry and to trust your plan for our lives. Amen.

29
Bifocals

———✖✖✖———

Scripture Reading: John 9:13-38

One thing I do know, that though I was blind, now I see.

John 9:25

A miracle happened.

Our ophthalmologist was reluctant to remove my husband's cataracts because the surgery requires holding the head in a specific position. Because Bob is missing three cervical vertebrae, a titanium plate and screws hold his head onto his body. His neck is rigid and bent severely forward. The doctor feared he could not properly align Bob's head with the surgical equipment. As the cataracts became progressively worse, Bob became increasingly depressed without his eyesight.

Finally the doctor's compassion for his patient overruled his fears about getting him into proper position, and he agreed to try. A clever nurse came up with a way to slant the bed and use pillows to achieve the necessary alignment, and everything proceeded smoothly. With the cataract removed and a new implant, Bob could see 20/20 for the first time in his life. His joy was immense. The jubilation doubled when the second surgery was equally successful. His quality of life improved dramatically. My husband could read the newspaper, do crossword puzzles, and once again examine his immense coin collection. His spirits soared.

Bob still needs eyeglasses for reading, and he continues to be obsessed with them. He now has four pairs, and he wants to know where they are at all times. I swear wee people live in this house and move the eyeglasses around, waiting for him to notice and complain loudly—the very moment I sit down at the computer to write.

Since eyeglasses hold major prominence in our daily existence, I was drawn to an excellent metaphor about having "bi-focal perceptions" of our care receivers. Robert L. DeWitt wrote a wise, tender, honest story about the growing presence of his wife's Alzheimer's disease in their long and loving marriage. In *Ebb Tide: An Encounter with Alzheimer's*, DeWitt writes about how the short-range lenses enable the caregiver to see the patient and the status of her physical and mental health exactly where she is situated at present. That up-close vision clarifies what needs to be done, as well as how and when to do it. The long-range lenses keep in focus who and what she was before the illness. The distant vision summons dignity and respect in the relationship.

———————————

Prayer: Lord God, Healer of the Blind, let me see my husband through bifocals: up close to discern how best to care for him in the present and far away so I may remember and respect the incredible human being who shares my life. Amen.

30
A Spacious Place

Scripture Reading: Psalm 66:8-12

We went through fire and through water;
yet you have brought us out to a spacious place.

Psalm 66:12

This was one of those glorious mornings with no doctor appointments or places we had to go. Devotion time was relaxed, unrushed. I let the words of the psalm flow over me. "Bless our God, O peoples, let the sound of his praise be heard, who has kept us among the living, and has not let our feet slip." God tested us, tried us, laid burdens on our backs, yet God brought us to "a spacious place."

The phrase remained with me as I walked our dog, Molly. That energetic little sheltie enjoys our outings so much she doesn't walk, trot, lumber, march, or amble. She prances during our forty-five minute promenades. It's quite fun to watch until a UPS truck passes by, and then she goes crazy, barking and pulling me in a ferocious chase down the street. This morning's walk was lovely—no trucks.

During our walk, I admired the cerulean sky and hazy cloud swirls overhead. I thought about "spaciousness." The biblical writers understood the universe to be composed of multiple dimensions and layers interconnected within the great cosmos. They held a comprehensive viewpoint of a Creator intimately involved in and with creation. If the ancients are correct, our existence is known to God. No one is insignificant to the Source—no one, not even caregivers who get angry and grumpy at times or slow, obstinate care receivers having a bad pain day. Our lives have purpose, meaning, and value to God.

This chain of connectedness among God, human beings, and the created order is expressed in a scene in Thornton Wilder's classic play *Our Town*. Young Rebecca looks out at the night sky, and asks her brother, "George, is the moon shining on South America, Canada, and half the whole world?"

"Well—prob'ly is."

Then thoughtfully, Rebecca tells him about an envelope addressed to a friend that located her in relation to the moon and the stars: " . . . Grover's Corners; Sutton County; New Hampshire; United States of America. . . . But listen, it's not finished: the United States of America; Continent of North America; Western Hemisphere; the Earth; the Solar System; the Universe; the Mind of God."

———————

Prayer: Source of all that is and ever shall be, you love us beyond our struggles and flaws and invite us into your spacious place. May the praises of your name echo throughout the universe. Amen.

31
Falsely Accused

─◆◆◆─

Scripture Reading: Ephesians 4:29–5:2

Be kind and compassionate to one another, forgiving each
other, just as in Christ God forgave you.

Ephesians 4:32

Last night when I went to Bob's office to tell him goodnight, he
said, "We've got to talk."

"Sure, what's on your mind?"

"I found out about you and your lover."

"What in the world are you talking about?"

"I heard you on the phone talking in whispers, but I could hear."

"No, you often don't hear correctly, especially without your
hearing aids. My cousin called to wish me happy birthday," I
said, while feeling totally exasperated.

"You're lying. I know what I heard, and I heard correctly this
time. You have a lover."

"Bob, why the heck would I do something stupid like that? I'm
tired and barely able to manage now without adding more compli-
cations. I love you, and I can assure you, you are enough man for
me." Under my breath, I muttered, "Much more than enough."

Then he abruptly concluded the conversation. "My emotions
are too raw. I don't want to talk about it anymore."

The human brain is complex and mysterious. When injury or
disease is added to the mix, predictability becomes even more elu-
sive. Bob has had episodes of suspiciousness before. He accused

a nurse's aide of stealing from his coin collection, and he still believes our grandson stole his switchblade even though we found the knife in question. He often accuses me of taking his wallet, eyeglasses, and other items when he has forgotten where he placed them.

A person with brain impairment who becomes "paranoid" has not gone crazy. Sometimes medications cause unrealistic ideas and hallucinations. I try to remember to separate Bob, the person, from the behavior he cannot control. But few things make me angrier than being falsely accused.

To further aggravate the situation, he can be quite normal and lucid, with an uncanny ability to get his act together for the doctor and family members. Based on what they observe, except for an occasional incongruent moment, he's doing great. Back home, Bob will slip back into occasional paranoia and forgetfulness. A suspicion may last for weeks or months even though I explain, write things down, or show him the "stolen" item. I'm still working on a way to convince him I have enough people in my life. I don't want any one else—certainly not a lover.

To tolerate something is to put up with it even though we dislike it. I tell myself—sometimes through clenched teeth—this paranoia is not important. I hope to go one step further toward accepting this stressful annoyance, to take my world as it is without sacrificing my serenity.

Prayer: Gracious God, we caregivers often face tough situations that aren't easily resolved. Grow in us a capacity for compassion, kindness, and forgiveness in the face of false accusations. Amen.

32
The Simple Life

⸎

Scripture Reading: Luke 12:27-34

For where your treasure is, there your heart will be also.

Luke 12:34

I have a long-standing habit of starting my daily meditation time with *Forward Day by Day*, a devotional booklet mailed to my house quarterly. Inside the front cover a "Morning Resolve" begins, "I will try this day to live a simple, sincere, and serene life." I've always been an orderly person ("a place for everything and everything in its place"). But over the years I have accumulated huge amounts of stuff. Orderliness and simplicity are not necessarily the same.

I cannot pinpoint the exact time or the specific reason that triggered a desire to live the "simple, sincere, and serene life," but some time ago I decided to head down that path. The first focus was simplicity. New houses, divorce, new jobs, downsizing, and Bob's failing health mandated a smaller-scale lifestyle. I elected not to hang onto things when other people could truly use and appreciate them. Anything that was not useful or especially meaning-filled left via garage sales and charity donations.

In addition to "Morning Resolve" and life situations, I found a cheerleader for the simple life in Sarah Ban Breathnach. She wrote a popular book in the mid-1990s titled *Simple Abundance*. I jot down favorite quotations on index cards and recently found this one from Breathnach:

As I wandered through the rooms of the house I began to search for the common thread in the lives of the world's great spiritual teachers and traditions: Jesus Christ, Mohammed, Buddha, Lao-Tzu, The Hebrew prophets, The Moslem Sufis, The Catholic saints, The Hindu rishis, The Shakers, The Quakers, The Amish. *None of them had junk drawers.* That's because all embraced simplicity. Spirituality, simplicity, and serenity seem to be a sacred trinity; three divine qualities of the orderly soul.

As a caregiver and companion to my chronically ill husband, I treasure the simple life. It is freeing to get rid of things. Curiously, the fewer the material possessions, the more content we become. Don't get the idea I have become a minimalist. I used to have five spatulas and now I have two. I may cut to one, but I'm not there yet. Facing mortality has led me to shift more attention to clutter that gums up the pipes of my relationship with God: Father, Son, and Spirit. I am eons from the spiritual saintliness of Italian poet and Franciscan lay brother Jacopone (1230–1306). He wrote another favorite index-card quotation: "Poverty is to have nothing and desire nothing; yet possessing everything."

Prayer: Lord of all and everything, you urge those of us caring for a loved one to find a simpler lifestyle both within and without. Show us how to simplify further, but please say it's okay to have at least one junk drawer. Amen.

33
Family Feud

━━━━━━━━

Scripture Reading: 2 Samuel 18:24-33

The king [David] was deeply moved, and went up to the chamber over the gate, and wept; and as he went, he said, "O my son Absalom, my son, my son Absalom!"

2 Samuel 18:33

At 4:00 in the morning the phone jarred me out of a deep sleep. The caller, who lives in Europe, asked to speak to his younger brother. Since this man sometimes miscalculates the time difference, I didn't give the call another thought and promptly went back to sleep. Later I learned about the importance of the call. The caller told Bob his family had admitted him to a facility a few days earlier. To say he was unhappy is an understatement. He was mad as a hornet's nest hit with a baseball bat.

Next his wife got on the phone and gave the other side of the story. Her husband had become combative. He had incontinence yet refused to allow his family to bathe him. He was falling constantly and required physical assistance that his tiny, frail wife could not provide. He became confused. Living conditions had deteriorated in their small third-floor apartment. It was beyond time for this man to go into nursing care. But the family feud remained intense.

As I listened to Bob recount the situation, I was reminded of the traumatized woman who attended our support group for the first time last month. She was forced to admit her husband to a facility after an eruption of belligerence and physical abuse. She struggled to locate permanent arrangements for his care. Her shock, pain, and bewilderment were blatant. She said, "I feel alone and scared." A group member responded quickly, "But you're not alone. You are here, and many of us have been through exactly what you are going through."

Another woman at the meeting spoke with resignation in her voice, "I'm not far behind you. My husband won't let me sleep in the bedroom anymore because he doesn't remember I'm his wife." Debilitating illnesses are responsible for many heart-breaking family feuds.

David may have been Israel's greatest king, but his family life was dysfunctional and tragic. For example, David's third son, Absalom, killed his own half-brother to avenge the rape of his sister, lived for years in exile, and then led a popular but unsuccessful uprising against his father. David's mournful cries of anguish on hearing the news of his son's death echo the pathos so many of us feel when family systems change and fall apart. Family dynamics are charged with emotions that surface and sometimes shock during crises.

Prayer: Unchanging, faithful God, nothing can guard us from heartache except an awareness of your presence. You are everything we need when we have nothing left. Amen.

34
Falling Down

Scripture Reading: Jude 20-25

Now to [God our Savior] who is able to keep you from falling . . . be glory, majesty, power, and authority, before all time and now and forever. Amen.

Jude 24a, 25b

The crisp Indian summer morning was perfect for walking Molly. Our four-year-old sheltie was excited when I brought out the leash. She tugged, pranced, and pulled as we went down the street at a quick pace (her choice, not mine).

Molly has an annoying habit of lunging and barking ferociously at big trucks—even with me attached to the other end of her leash. This "perfect" morning's walk was going happily when a UPS truck approached from behind. At the exact moment it passed us, Molly made a quick circle around me and then ran full speed toward the truck. I felt the leash tighten around my ankles, and over I went, falling hard to the ground.

The driver stopped his truck and started toward us. Molly's barking became louder, and she started to growl, so I told him I was okay and asked him to leave. More surprising than my not breaking any bones was the fact I didn't let go of the leash—especially with the pain Molly's lunging exacerbated in what turned out to be a sprained wrist and three bent, swelling fingers.

My knee, shoulder, and hip were also hurt, but we managed to complete a shortened walk. A long soak in a warm bath helped, but I hurt then and still did several days later. A wrist brace provided stability but was cumbersome and led to everyone asking what happened. I have endured my husband's tales of bad falls and physical woes for years and truly find the subject, even when my own, quite tiresome.

The interesting part of the story is what I thought about when the accident happened. Words from a song on a Donnie McClurkin CD popped into my head: "We fall down, but we get up; we fall down, but we get up. For a saint is just a sinner who fell down, and got up."

Caregiving, as well as sin, jerks us off our feet into the dirt of despair, loneliness, and anger. But we don't have to stay there, because God has provided an unbreakable, permanent foundation of forgiveness when we slip into lack of trust and self-pity. We need only to grasp the hand God offers and hold on like a trusting child. God will help us get to our feet. We are loved and always forgiven; we need only to claim God's gifts.

———————————

Prayer: Forgiving God, I approach you this morning limping, hurting and weighed down. I know you rescue the fallen. Come, Lord, and lead us struggling caregivers home. Amen.

35
A Good Book

Scripture Reading: Revelation 1:1-8

*Blessed is the one who reads aloud the words of the prophecy,
and blessed are those who hear and who keep
what is written in it.*

Revelation 1:3

Like Belle in the Disney version of *Beauty and the Beast*, I am called a "bibliophile," a lover of books. I started reading at age three, and I remain a voracious reader, although I have become more selective. The fact that I became a librarian surprised no one. When my husband became seriously ill, I had to retire from my job as a children's librarian in a large municipal public library system. I missed the people, but the toughest withdrawal was leaving all those books.

My husband's diseases took a huge toll on his eyes. His depression from being unable to read, do crossword puzzles, examine his coins, and see well enough for simple tasks broke my heart. I could not imagine the difficulty and despair that problem would create for me. Armed with dogged determination, again we went to the best ophthalmologist we could find. This doctor listened to the desperation in Bob's voice and set a date for the first surgery. The success of the implant was phenomenal, and the second surgery brought equally transformative results. The radical improvement in the quality of my husband's life was miraculous.

Life is like a good book. There are countless times when we don't have the foggiest understanding about what's happening. We puzzle over how the characters, the plot, themes, and episodes fit into the story. We read on, trusting that everything will make sense in the end. We believe somehow times of fear, bewilderment, and confusion will change to wonder, grace, and revelation when we have reached the concluding words. In the meantime, we read on. We simply show up, walk humbly with our God, and anticipate the next chapter of our life story.

The first of seven beatitudes, or blessings, in the opening verses of Revelation reminds us that God's story blesses. Blessed is the one who reads, the one who hears, and the one who keeps the words of the scriptures. I add my own benediction today: blessed is the one who finds hope in the Word even when brokenhearted, depressed, oppressed, or blind.

———————

Prayer: Great God of Creation and Author of the Scriptures, thank you for the blessings of good books and the Good Book. Amen.

36
The Gardener

～

Scripture Reading: Psalm 92:12-15

In old age they still produce fruit;
they are always green and full of sap.

Psalm 92:14

This reading from the Psalter is part of a hymn of thanksgiving for the greatness of God's works. The psalm bears the designation "A Song for the Sabbath Day," the only psalm so designated in the Hebrew text of the Psalter. There is incredible wisdom in a seven-day design that includes a day for rest and worship.

My grandfather owned a large farm where work was never-ending, yet he and his workers followed the sabbath rule. The one exception I remember as a child was that someone had to milk the cow on Sunday. The rhythm of the week flowed naturally into a rhythm of months and seasons. Granddaddy kept his life in tune with those cycles. Certain crops had to be planted on Good Friday and others harvested before the first frost. Timing was critical. When he was blessed with good weather and plentiful harvests, he had a spring in his step and a smile in his heart.

I am neither farmer nor botanist like others in my family, but I always have a few flowerbeds, even if I'm living in rental property. When the drab days of winter are almost over, the gardening bug bites me. I skip out to play in the dirt. Pulling dead leaves and dried-up plants out of flowerbeds is invigorating. The discovery of new buds and multiplied perennials is exhilarating.

Dividing and making new garden spots with my multiples or giving some away gladdens something deep within me.

I love gardening and have learned it is one hobby that cheers my care receiver, my neighbors, and me. No matter how complex Bob's health issues become or how confined to home we are, I can find an hour or two to putter in the garden.

Today's scripture verses contrast the temporary success of the wicked with the achievements of the righteous (people who desire a right relationship with God and others). The righteous are like the palm tree and the cedar in Lebanon, symbols of prosperity and longevity. The only hope I have to attain righteousness is to ask God to be the gardener of my soul. I close with a lovely prayer by Richard Foster.

––––––––––––––

Prayer:
Spirit of the living God, be the Gardener of my soul. For so long I have been waiting, silent and still—experiencing a winter of the soul. But now, in the strong name of Jesus Christ, I dare to ask:

> Clear away the dead growth of the past,
> Break up the hard clods of custom and routine,
> Stir in the rich compost of vision and challenge,
> Bury deep in my soul the implanted Word,
> Cultivate and water and tend my heart,
> Until new life buds and opens and flowers.
> Amen.

37
Friend

Scripture Reading: John 15:12-17

You are my friends if you do what I command you.

John 15:14

The interdenominational organization called Stephen Ministry equips persons to provide free, confidential, Christian, one-on-one care to those who are experiencing some form of life crisis. A Stephen Minister is prayerfully assigned after he or she has completed fifty hours of initial training and agreed to participate in ongoing group supervision and skill building. This program takes church members' needs seriously and provides a venue for the expression of God's care and love.

My husband was familiar with Stephen Ministry since I have been a Stephen Minister for a decade. During a meeting three years ago, a member asked if I thought Bob would like to have a Stephen Minister. In a matter of weeks, Bob and Danny began to develop one of the most incredible friendships I've witnessed.

People have spiritual as well as emotional and physical needs. Bob is obviously physically challenged and uses a walker or motorized chair. Danny takes Bob to breakfast at a neighborhood café some Saturday mornings. He is gentle and patient with his slow-as-molasses care receiver and intensely watches Bob's movements. Danny doesn't get upset with food and coffee spills. He lets Bob take the lead when they pray together.

Danny's major gift is the hours and hours of listening even

though Bob gets confused and says the same things many times over. These two men have long telephone conversations. Sometimes Bob falls asleep, but Danny has learned to simply hang up after a period without responses. The generosity of this man even led him to enlist his son to help with our move.

Three or four times Bob and Danny have ventured out with the metal detector, and on one of their excursions they found a lost high school class ring. I think Bob would find satisfaction and fulfillment even if they went to the food market to watch folks bag groceries, simply because he was with his kind and trustworthy friend.

Jesus' command to love one another is being lived out in the relationship of these two strong Christian men. I thank Danny often, and occasionally I bake him a cake. I believe he has played a major role in Bob's being alive and content today. Billy Graham appeared on the *Today Show* decades ago, and I heard him say, "Religion picks up where psychology leaves off." Bob may be coping with raw emotions, stresses, and chronic pain, but he does not need a psychiatrist. He has Jesus and Jesus' friend Danny.

I know firsthand that Stephen Ministers make loving friends for caregivers too.

Prayer: Good and Gracious God, thank you for your friends who serve as faith-filled, grace-filled, compassionate Stephen Ministers. Amen.

38
How Much to Tell

—∞∞∞—

Scripture Reading: James 1:2-5

If any of you is lacking in wisdom, ask God, who gives to all generously and ungrudgingly, and it will be given you.

James 1:5

Something had been troubling me, and I expected to find guidance somewhere in my growing stack of caregiver educational books and magazines. But to my dismay not one mention of my dilemma was found. Surely there are caregivers wrestling with this worrisome issue of how much to tell family, friends, support group members, and others. How much should I reveal about my husband's diseases, his behavior, our daily lives, and our foibles?

While in the office making copies of recipes for the twice-baked potatoes and brisket we had for Father's Day dinner, I told daughter Jill about going to her dad's neurologist. Dr. Smith ordered several tests and phoned us with the results of the CAT scan recently made of Bob's head. More tests will be done next week. An increase in myoclonic seizures prompted this latest flurry of tests. I reassured Jill nothing was seriously changed, and the doctor said not to worry. Later I wondered if I should have told her anything at all. I bet she went right home to learn everything she could about myoclonus on the Internet.

Each family system is unique, and the dynamics within the system vary for each individual family member. Jill and husband, Joe, live in the same town with us. The other four children live in four other states, and we are surprised if we get to see them once or twice a year. Location and accessibility naturally define which child becomes the predominant helper. Jill loves her father deeply. Both she and her husband are compassionate, loving people who want to be involved. They provide solid, dependable, bedrock support for Bob and me. I do not know where we would be without them.

My struggle involves how much to disclose to Jill, the children, friends, family members, those of you reading this book. While I don't want to breach Bob's privacy, I know it is important for those who help us with personal matters to know the facts. What needs to be confidential? What needs to be shared? To whom should I disclose what? What do I expect will happen once the information is given? Will what I disclose be uplifting, encouraging and edifying, or hurtful and unwanted? The questions persist.

The best I can do is pray—pray for discretion in my choices of disclosure. Perhaps the comment of a member of the support group provides useful advice: "The healthiest families have the fewest secrets."

_____

Prayer: Come, Holy Spirit, and give the gift of wisdom to those of us who care for a loved one. May we discern how much to tell and when we need to remain silent. Amen.

39
Cheerios

Scripture Reading: Ecclesiastes 2:24-25; Psalm 34:8

*There is nothing better for mortals than to eat and drink,
and find enjoyment in their toil. . . . for apart from [God]
who can eat or who can have enjoyment?*

Ecclesiastes 2:24-25

This morning I felt sorry for myself as I dragged my aging body out of bed. My husband had a doctor's appointment twenty miles away. He wanted to get a haircut afterward. I had to drive to another doctor's office to pick up his prescription (which must be hand delivered to the pharmacy) and deposit it with the pharmacist on the other side of town. Bob needed fresh bananas to help him swallow his meds. I needed to purchase a grandson's birthday card and mail today so it would not be late. I was aware the mopey munchies had struck again and were gobbling up my joy like a horde of grasshoppers ravaging a wheat field.

When I was seated for breakfast with Bob, I looked down at my bowl of Cheerios and fresh blueberries. Little, round, brown Os and shiny navy blue orbs floated in a milky puddle right before my eyes. Granules of unwashed Turbinado sugar, harvested from 100 percent sugar cane, glistened on top of the cereal and berries. A ray of filtered sunlight from the window danced above the yellow bowl. I studied what was in front of me and soon forgot about everything else. I became enchanted with the delightful aliveness of my ordinariness.

90

I asked Bob whether his children, my amazing stepchildren, enjoyed Cheerios the way my three did when they were very young. We recalled chubby toddler fingers developing manual dexterity as our little people learned how to pick up tiny Os and bits of cheese from a high chair tray. We exchanged memories of cute and touching things our children did and in the sharing celebrated our extravagant blessings.

Our reading today comes from Ecclesiastes, a word from the Greek translation of the Hebrew title, *Qoheleth*, the Teacher. The word *vanity* appears often in the book and has been translated incorrectly "meaninglessness," "absurd," and "useless." The literal meaning of *habel*, often translated "vanity," is "breath" or "breeze," something hard to grasp. The Teacher uses this term as a metaphor for the transience, tensions, and contradictions of life.

Qoheleth, an utter realist, asks what good can come from a life of toil and strain (2:22). In a modestly positive answer, he encourages his readers to take pleasure in what they're doing now—to enjoy life because it comes from God's hand. Those who discover a purpose in life take each day as a gift from God, thank God for it, and serve God in it.

Prayer: Lord God, fount of wisdom and meaning, I praise you for Cheerios and blueberries and the gift of another day with my loved one. May we caregivers never forget to notice and appreciate the extraordinary ordinary blessings you provide here and now. Amen.

40
The Folded Napkin

Scripture Reading: John 20:1-10

*[Simon Peter] saw the linen wrappings lying there, and the
cloth that had been on Jesus' head, not lying with the linen
wrappings but rolled up in a place by itself.*

John 20:6b-7

The Lord gifted me with the opportunity to facilitate three
weekly adult Bible classes. Delving into scripture, commen-
taries, and Bible resources in preparation, and then leading people who seek to know and serve the Lord better, pulls me out of
my isolation and caregiving challenges. When engaged in this
activity of shared faith formation, I feel I am walking on holy
ground.

Today I meditated on a fact one of the students pointed out. It
appears in the Resurrection story in the Gospel of John. Up until
that time, I had not noticed the detail about the napkin that had
covered Jesus' head in the burial tomb. It was folded and lying to
the side away from the other cast-off linen wrappings.

This custom has significance in the light of Hebrew tradition
regarding a servant's relationship to the master. Once a servant
set the dinner table, he retreated out of sight while the master ate.
At the conclusion of the meal, the master would rise, wipe his
fingers and mouth, and clean his beard. If he crumpled up the
napkin and tossed it on the table, the servant knew the master
was finished. But if the master got up from the table, folded the

napkin, and laid it beside his plate, the servant knew not to touch the table; the rolled cloth meant "I'm coming back."

The symbolism of this small detail triggered a reflection and subsequent connection to caregiving. Caregivers find themselves in a servant role, learning about the truth of crucifixion of self, both found and required, in caregiving. Not always but some days I feel trapped in a tomb of low-grade panic, weariness, grubbiness, and fear. This place is dark, cold, lonely, endless.

As I meditate, my heart-eyes adjust to the cave darkness. In the corner, I see a folded napkin that rouses me from my state of mere survival. Love overcomes death, dirt, drudgery. A miracle happens and changes me—heals my heart of losses, fears, and exhaustion. Real Love, not simplistic love like duty to care for my husband but Love from the Most High Holy, transcends ego and encourages me to embrace and cherish my caregiver role. Caring for Bob is crucial to my spiritual journey, because it leads me to enter deeper into the self-breaking blessing of the Love and Light of the Servant Master. Caregiving carries me into the tomb but does not leave me there until I have found the napkin of hope.

Prayer: Gracious God of New Life, help us to hold the folded napkin and accept your invitation to show up every day with expectant eyes that can see your miracles amongst the meals, the laundry, and the bounden duties. Thank you for coming back and showing us Love wins in the end. Amen.

41
Under Their Feet

Scripture Reading: Psalm 30

God, the Lord, is my strength;
he makes my feet like hinds' feet,
he makes me tread upon my high places.

Habakkuk 3:19, RSV

The morning routine went well today: got Molly out for her constitutional, took and recorded husband's glucose count, gave him his insulin shot, and watched him consume his pile of pills without difficulty. I fixed his favorite, simple breakfast—oatmeal with one pack of Splenda, two tablespoons of chopped walnuts, and four tablespoons of milk. He knows what he likes, and that certainly beats having to guess. He is settled now at the table with a crossword puzzle.

I pour another cup of coffee and scurry into the guest room where I have my comfy armchair, a reading lamp, and a wobbly homemade bookcase. In the small duplex where we now live, there is no room for my "prayer corner" in the master bedroom. But the current arrangement works well since visitors are rare.

Placing my big pottery mug on a coaster, I arrange the butterfly needlework pillow behind my back. I light a candle and begin prayers and daily readings. This turns out to be a good day—only two minor interruptions during my meditations. It occurs to me that I am now able to distinguish good and bad days. For months and months all days seemed sad, stressful, and crazy. This day, this moment, I feel God's strength giving me the agility of a deer: I ascend from the silences of personal despair to a high place of renewed life and hope.

The feeling reminds me of a profound little story written in 1955 by Hannah Hurnard, *Hinds' Feet on High Places*. The book is allegory that expresses the desire to be led to love, joy, and victory. The plot follows Much-Afraid on her spiritual journey with her companions, Sorrow and Suffering. She overcomes tormenting fears to reach, at last, the High Places where she gains a new name, Grace and Glory. Her communion with the loving Shepherd transforms her and then sends her back to the valley renewed and confident.

Life experiences have led me to believe it is the obstacles we, with God's help, have to transcend that bring out the best in us. Poet Emily Dickinson said it this way, "A wounded deer leaps highest." James Oppenheim spelled out the thought even more dynamically, saying that the foolish seek happiness in the distance, while the wise grow it under their feet.

———————————

Prayer: Teach us, O God, to take the gift of a day and give it back to you. Help us walk in radiant faith and loyal service with heightened awareness that moments of spontaneous joy can be found here in the valley right under our feet. Amen.

42
Thin Places

———

Scripture Reading: Exodus 3:1-6

*Then [God] said, "Come no closer! Remove the sandals from
your feet, for the place on which you are
standing is holy ground."*

Exodus 3:5

As a young girl, I loved walks in the woods surrounding the
family farm in south Mississippi. I had a favorite spot where a
sweet gum tree grew up straight two feet, took a sharp ninety-
degree turn parallel to the ground for three feet, made another
sharp ninety-degree turn, then reached straight up toward the
sky. I believed God made the tree especially for me. I liked to sit
on the bend with my legs folded up to my chest and my back resting on the trunk.

In the overhead leafy bower, I watched sun rays dance in the
dappled air. Birdcalls seemed louder there. A cold artesian spring
fed a nearby stream. In March and April rare white violets covered the brook's banks. I formed whimsical ideas about animals
and wee people living in "my special place." While there, I felt a
deep connection to the Lord God. No one told me, but I knew the
first time I wandered into this place that it was "holy ground."

The Celtic tradition has a phrase for places like this; they are
called "thin places." In simple terms "thin place" describes a spot
where the veil separating heaven and earth is like a porous net.
"Thin place" experiences have been so powerful that I have

discovered memories of them can provide ports during stressful, stormy days.

I often recall a small outdoor chapel on a wooded hillside in the North Carolina mountains with its log pews and altar inscribed with the St. Francis Prayer. The chapel and the bent tree are two stopping places where I pause to remember the closeness of the Other and to find comfort in the midst of grief, trials, and boredom of daily life. My spaces open a pathway connected to something greater—that something capable of satisfying unknown yearnings and hungers.

I believe there are "thin-place people" as well as "thin places." I know people so full of God's love, they leak it everywhere they go. Often my husband has a deep, quiet inner peace like a thin-place person. I am profoundly grateful for the faith lodged deep in his soul that supports him in his suffering. Traveling this path of chronic illness and caregiving is not easy. We both hurt. But we also have found thin places and thin-place people that startle us and bless us with gifts of grace.

———————

Prayer: O God, may we willingly step into our particular woods, stand still, breathe deep, and open our spirits to you. May we become thin-place people leaking Love to those who need it. Amen.

43
Better, Not Bitter

Scripture Reading: Psalm 73:21-28

When my soul was embittered,
when I was pricked in heart,
I was stupid and ignorant.

Psalm 73:21-22

Years ago the disorientation and heartache of divorce after twenty-seven years of marriage led me to attend a Divorce Recovery seminar offered at a local church. Lectures, videos, workbooks, and small sharing groups were educational and helpful. Surprisingly, the most beneficial aid of that eight-week course came during one of the breaks. Eddie, the facilitator of my small group, handed me a cup of coffee and sat down next to me on the brick wall. His words are permanently etched into my psyche.

"We've been coming to these sessions for almost two months now. You've been open and honest and an eager student. You are a lovely woman and a special lady. I hope you will take what I am about to say in the way it is intended. Nell, please don't become bitter like so many divorcées. Please use this experience to become better."

My reaction was indignation, hurt, and shock. Eddie had nailed me. Like the psalmist, I was "embittered" with a "pricked heart." After that kind of candid exposure, there was no excuse to remain stupid and ignorant. The time had arrived for me to get good counsel and develop a plan for my spiritual healing and growth.

Upon examination, my image of God was shallower and more superficial than I cared to admit (except in my darkest, rawest hours). A moral inventory motivated a burning desire to mature into a better disciple for the Lord. I wanted to be an authentic Christian. With the passage of time, I drew closer to the Mystery I call God. That movement of soul inched me toward a bigger capacity to love, forgive, and respect others. The bitterness crept away gradually.

Eddie's words remain my plumb line. Two years after Bob and I married, Bob's health took a nosedive. I was angry and disoriented again. Life was not going the way it was supposed to. Disappointment engulfed me, and I was reeling once more. In my experience, every life crisis brings with it a spiritual crisis. The time had returned for the "better, not bitter" self-examination and wise counsel.

Occasionally a slip into bitterness and self-pity occurs, but it never lasts long. Eddie's lesson was tough, and I can't forget it for long. I stumble on ever so slowly toward a vision of a "better" me and a "better" world. God forbid I ever become a bitter caregiver.

Prayer: God of Love, my will is to do your will. Guide those of us called into the ministry of caregiving to the holy vision you hold for us. Amen.

44
My New Best Friend

Scripture Reading: Romans 5:1-5

Hope does not disappoint us, because God's love has been poured into our hearts through the Holy Spirit that has been given to us.

Romans 5:5

"**W**hat helped you get through those years during your wife's illness? You even arranged for her to stay home until she died. How did you do it?"

I sat with my wise, white-haired spiritual director in his study. My questions were not meant to be intrusive; they just came rolling out. Weeks before this remarkable man was to retire, his wife was diagnosed with Alzheimer's disease. He spent the first years of his retirement being caregiver and nurse. He learned about cooking meals, household maintenance, women's clothing, laundry, children's affairs, and other duties a traditional wife typically handles.

As caregivers, we had discussed feelings of loss, disappointment, isolation, and anger. My questions asked nothing about the prayer life or support system of this deeply faithful man of God. I wanted to know what he discovered when the soul is stripped of everyone and everything. When you are empty, what helps you keep going?

"Nell, I don't know what I would have done without my journals. I wrote my feelings, details about what was happening to my wife, reactions of family and friends, any and everything that popped into my mind. Journaling helped me get through."

I understood his answer; I have kept journals for twenty-three years. A journal is not a diary, although it may include diary-like notations about happenings and everyday details. The distinguishing factor of journaling is the invitation to go inward. You record what you find during your interior heart-mind meanderings. You write what bubbles up from inside. The process cultivates honesty and authenticity.

Only the author reads a journal, whereas a diary seems to anticipate someone may find and read it. A journal is like a new best friend. Nothing will ever be repeated to someone else. You can let it all hang out. You won't be judged, and you won't hurt anyone's feelings. You can trust its confidentiality.

When I sit down with journal and pen, I light a candle and pray: "Come, Holy Spirit; enlighten the hearts of the faithful." I try to empty my mind and let whatever is inside reveal itself. Often I am sad, angry, struggling. As I write, something intriguing happens. By the time I record whatever needs to surface, I feel release. I experience a metamorphosis that unleashes a powerful awareness of God's love. Keeping a journal is like walking down a path to God.

———

Prayer: Holy Spirit, thank you for the practice of journal writing where God's love can pour into my heart. May that love overflow into what I say and do for others today. Amen.

45
Forgiving Hearts

Scripture Reading: Colossians 3:12-15

Just as the Lord has forgiven you, so you also must forgive.

Colossians 3:13b

In the October 19, 2007 issue of *United Methodist Reporter,* I found an intriguing article about how a community has handled tragedy. One year earlier, a milk truck driver had entered a one-room school in Nickel Mines, Pennsylvania, and shot ten little girls before killing himself. The four Amish families who lost five children are learning to navigate their grief one difficult step at a time. Caring people—both Amish and English (the term the Amish use for "outsiders")—responded with food, prayers, cards, gifts, and over $4.3 million in donations to a fund for the families. A new school opened in the fall of 2007.

A farmer who lost two daughters knew his intense grief was lifting when he became interested in working in the fields again. Another father said he understood things were changing when "it didn't hurt like it did at four months." Three families who lost children have had babies since the shootings. I was touched to learn that one little boy asked his mother if his sisters up in heaven helped to pick out the new baby for their family. According to the report, his mother expressed her faith this way: "There's a rainbow after each storm; that's what keeps us moving." The living siblings have also kept the parents moving, as have the love and support of others.

These families, bound by a common painful experience, have drawn close. One mother commented about their bond: "I don't know how it would feel if we had been the only ones. We have each other to come together and share."

In the weeks after the murders, the world was stunned by the Amish families' grace toward the killer and his family. What people witnessed in their behavior was a faith principle already in their hearts and minds. They believe that as Jesus forgives them, so they must forgive others and they strive to live by that ideal.

The reporters wrote about one father who said that when he and his wife "released" the murderer, they were released from anger and bitterness but not from pain. His wife softly added, "Just because you've forgiven doesn't mean you've forgotten, or that it doesn't hurt."

This powerful story reminds me that caregivers need one another too. People need people, especially during life experiences of loss, survival, and challenges of faith. We can encourage ourselves and others to remember that the love of God in Jesus Christ transforms hearts and minds, even in nightmarish circumstances.

———————

Prayer: Gracious God, help us by your Holy Spirit to love as Christ loved, that our lives may find a simple harmony with your purposes. Amen.

46
Attaboy

—⊶⊷—

Scripture Reading: 1 Thessalonians 5:8-11

*Therefore encourage one another and build up each other,
as indeed you are doing.*

1 Thessalonians 5:11

This week a card arrived in the mail for Bob from two women in our church family. A printed poem conveyed wishes for a lightened heart and peaceful moments and conveyed loving thoughts. As lovely as the sentiments printed on the card were, it was the handwritten note that tugged vigorously at my husband's psyche and brought a smile to his heart.

> Dear Bob,
> Hope this card finds you in minimal pain today. Take care and know that you are a great witness to others of a strong Christian faith.

Bob looked up over his reading glasses and asked, "Do people really think about me that way? We go to church every Sunday, but I didn't know anyone noticed an old man in a wheelchair. I feel humbled."

Everyone craves a pat on the back, an "Attaboy" for good work or special behavior. Heartfelt, authentic praise, without ulterior motive, brightens faces and lifts hearts. We all go through life wondering if we're good enough or have value, and I suspect the chronically ill need genuine affirmations more than anyone.

Their self-esteem is tied into what they can do and accomplish, and now their debilitation makes them think they are useless, dispensable.

Bob sometimes expresses a feeling of worthlessness. He believes he is a burden on me and on his family. I praise him and encourage him, but the depth of a spouse's acknowledgment doesn't register in the way someone else's kind words can. A healthy spouse's praises might be taken as exaggeration or manipulation. The message in Bob's card was unquestionably *other*-oriented. Bob became a bit teary-eyed when he read the words. They had a generous, therapeutic value.

Charles M. Schwab (1862–1939), American industrialist, president of Carnegie Steel Company and later Bethlehem Steel, made this statement: "I have yet to find the man, however great or exalted his station, who did not do better work and put forth greater effort under a spirit of approval than he would ever do under a spirit of criticism. . . . The way to develop the best that is in a man is by appreciation and encouragement."

Our words of sincere esteem may seem insignificant, but they can touch someone deeply. Bob's reaction reminded me I too could send cards and e-mail or phone people with expressions of admiration and care.

Prayer: Thank you, Loving God, for the inspiration we find in faith that sustains those enduring pain and illness. Teach us care providers, Lord, to be a blessing to others by offering them words of appreciation and encouragement. Amen.

47

The Cracked Pot

Scripture Reading: Isaiah 64:6-8

Yet, O Lord, you are our father;
we are the clay, and you are our potter;
we are all the work of your hand.

Isaiah 64:8

Years ago I heard what I considered a trivial story at the time. I misjudged, though, because it often comes to mind when my behavior is flawed and my emotions are flustered. I recently rediscovered the story on the Internet. It goes like this:

A water bearer in India had two large pots that hung on the end of a pole that he carried across his neck. One pot was perfect and always delivered a full portion of water at the end of the long walk from the stream to the master's house. The other pot had a crack in it and arrived at the house half full.

The perfect pot was quite proud of its accomplishments, perfect to the purpose for which it was made. The poor cracked pot was ashamed of its imperfection and miserable about only doing half of what it was made to do.

For two years, the water bearer daily delivered only one and a half pots of water. The cracked pot felt like a bitter failure and one day told the bearer, "I am ashamed of myself, and want to apologize to you."

"Why?" asked the bearer. "What are you ashamed of?"

"Because of my flaws you have to work harder, and you don't get full value from your efforts," lamented the pot.

The water bearer said, "As we return to the master's house, I want you to notice the beautiful flowers along the path."

As they went up the hill, the old cracked pot observed lovely, colorful wild flowers on the side of the path. But it still felt bad because it had leaked out half its load. Again the old pot apologized for its failure.

The bearer said, "Did you notice there were flowers only on your side of the path? I have always known about your flaw and I planted flower seeds on your side. Every day when we walked back from the stream, you've watered them. For two years, I have picked beautiful flowers to decorate my master's table. Without you being just the way you are, he would not have this beauty to grace his home."

Many think it is humility to say they do little and have small value. We caregivers feel like what we do is mundane and unimportant. But we are like a little leaky pot. It is not the pot (me, self, ego) but the water, the Spirit of the living God, passing through us that blesses.

Prayer: Great Potter, may our care receivers recognize their help comes not from their caregivers but from your Spirit flowing through them. Thank you for allowing us clay pots to bring beauty to grace our Master's table. Amen.

48
A Walk in the Park

Scripture Reading: Matthew 6:25-34

And can any of you by worrying add a single hour to your span of life?

Matthew 6:27

Our dog, Molly, was driving us crazy with her scratching. Apparently she picked up fleas either on a walk or while being boarded when we attended our granddaughter's college graduation. It was a toss-up as to whether Molly or Bob suffered the most. One day I decided to put them out of their misery. I carried Molly to the veterinarian.

She calmly took her cortisone shot and stood perfectly still while I observed how to apply monthly anti-flea medicine. The vet explained there would be no long-term benefits if I failed to get the exterminator to treat the house and yard for fleas. I went home and scheduled the pest control technician to come in three days. He advised us to leave the house for at least two hours after he sprayed.

I worried about the impact of this flea business on the monthly budget. Then I worried where to take a frolicsome four-year-old sheltie and a sedentary old man in a wheelchair. Malls were out of the question. Molly likes to jump up and kiss everyone. She's quite a leaper, so even six-footers are not safe from her slobbery greetings. Babies in strollers love her because her tongue tickles when she gives them soggy smooches. The good news is Molly loves people; the bad news is she loves too exuberantly.

For twenty-four hours I fretted about what to do with this pair until I remembered how much Molly and I enjoyed Village Creek Historical Recreation Area about three miles from home. We walked there a few times last spring. I invited Bob to join us on several occasions, but he always declined. This time I didn't ask. I loaded up drinks and a small bowl for Molly's water.

The wide, smooth, concrete walkways perfectly accommodate bikes, roller blades, strollers, *and* wheelchairs. The looping trail allows users to easily shorten or lengthen their excursions. And the heavily shaded path meets our need to keep Bob from over-exposure to the sun.

This rural Mississippi gal loves the woods, but we learned during that family outing—to our surprise—city slicker Bob does too. He grinned while he tested the speed of his motorized chair. When we stopped to rest and enjoy our drinks, Molly jumped up and sat on the bench. She lapped up her cool water and soon tugged at the leash to go again.

———————————

Prayer: Gracious God, why do I waste energy worrying? The fleas are gone. The stroll in the park was a blessing. When we human beings let you be in charge, the route we walk in life is never difficult or dreary. Today and always you provide tender light and restful shade as we walk our Path with you. Amen.

49
How Beautiful the Feet

──❀──

Scripture Reading: Romans 10:14-18

*And how are they to proclaim him unless they are sent? As it
is written, "How beautiful are the feet of
those who bring good news!"*

Romans 10:15

The youth group and several adults in my church embark on
mission and choir trips during the summer. This Sunday was designated Mission Sunday, when several team members talked
about their experiences during morning worship. The exuberance and gratitude for the opportunity to serve others shone on
their faces and in their words.

One team had been assigned the task of gutting a home in the
ninth ward of New Orleans, a neighborhood flooded when the lev-
ees broke during Hurricane Katrina. The house had been beneath
ten feet of water. Everything had been lost. The major work assignment was to remove molded Sheetrock and rotten wood.

The house is owned by an eighty-year-old widow; she had lost
her husband two months before the hurricane hit. She was
thrilled about the arrival of these Christian teens and their adult
helpers. Even though the team would be there only one week,
another team would follow, and another, until her residence was
rebuilt and she could return home.

The client showed her appreciation by furnishing doughnuts
and juice every morning. She learned about the group's devotions

at noon, joined them, and even shared bits of her faith story. The woman had retired from nursing at age sixty-five and joined the Peace Corps. She told them she was assigned to Jamaica, a place hotter in the summer than New Orleans. She came to loathe the long steamy walks to and from her job site until one morning when she became aware of the Lord's presence. She spoke to him, "Jesus, if you can walk the dusty road up the hills of Calvary for me, then I can walk up these Jamaican hills for you."

After the talks during worship, I listened to the powerful voice of our choir director sing "How Beautiful" by Twila Paris, a contemporary Christian songwriter, pianist, author, and recording artist. The words seeped into the seams of my soul:

> How beautiful the hands that served
> the wine and the bread and the sons of the earth;
> how beautiful the feet that walked
> the long dusty roads and the hill to the cross; . . .
> how beautiful when humble hearts give
> the fruit of pure lives so that others may live . . .
> how beautiful the feet that bring
> the sound of good news and the love of the King . . .
> how beautiful . . .

Mission trips, medical professionals, Peace Corps volunteers, helpers old and young, all reach out to assist others in need and thereby share the love of Christ. Caregivers too have "beautiful hands that serve" and "beautiful feet that bring the love of the King."

───────────

Prayer: Lord Jesus Christ, may we develop softened, grateful hearts that learn to cherish our caregiving opportunities to walk in your footsteps. Amen.

50
The Silversmith

Scripture Reading: Malachi 3:1-4

[The Lord] will sit as a refiner and purifier of silver; he will purify the Levites and refine them like gold and silver.

Malachi 3:3a, NIV

During our weekly Bible class, a member shared an e-mail she had received from a friend. It was one of those anonymous Christian messages that range from trite to profound. I liked this one. Here is the story:

> A woman in a Bible study became intrigued with the scripture passage found in Malachi 3:3 about the Lord sitting and refining silver. She decided to learn the deeper meaning behind the passage by visiting a silversmith. Kathy watched the smith hold the vat of raw metal in the hottest part of the fire until it melted. The impurities separated from the silver and rose to the surface where they were skimmed off, leaving the pure metal.
>
> As the worker skimmed off the impurities, Kathy asked him, "Do you always have to sit and watch the process?"
>
> "Oh, yes, I can't take my eyes off it until it is done."
>
> "How do you know when it is done?"
>
> "That's easy. It's done when I can see my reflection in it."

The prophet Malachi rebuked the people and priests of fifth-century BCE Israel for their unfaithfulness. But he also informed them God wants to restore a relationship with these wayward, disobedient children. The consequence of their [and our] willfulness and flirtation with lesser gods would be like a stint in a red-hot fire. But the refining process offers possibility for repentance, forgiveness, and purification. God is a compassionate silversmith eager to dispense second chances and healing love.

I threw a hissy fit this morning and needed a second chance. The depth of frustration had me sitting in a chair shaking, crying, and despairing. It was crazy and embarrassing. For weeks I had planned and carved out time to resume my devotional writing. I was behind schedule and unsure there were any more devotions left in me.

The fit was precipitated by Bob's unexpected request to go to the doctor (turns out he passed a kidney stone and had a urinary tract infection). He also requested an unplanned trip to the vet with our miserable, scratching dog.

Following the fit, I went to my prayer chair, settled down into a surprising calm, and afterward managed my responsibilities well. A period of silence with the Lord changes me every time. Will I never learn to graciously accept the disruptive circumstances of my life? They provide the heat that refines. Too bad I can't enjoy the smelting process. It invites the blessing of compassion.

Prayer: Refiner of Human Hearts, you are willing to take time to sit and transform us when we have our meltdowns. May we become pure enough for you to see your reflection in us more and more. Amen.

51
Winter Nest

Scripture Reading: John 14:15-23

*Jesus answered him, "Those who love me will keep my word,
and my Father will love them, and we will come to them and
make our home with them."*

John 14:23

The cold wind pinched my cheeks and stung my forehead as I
walked the dog. My eyes teared and my red nose dripped uncon-
trollably as Molly set a vigorous pace. My gloved fingers felt
numb as I fumbled for a tissue. Molly marched happily along in
her thick furry coat, but I was miserable. The chilly air froze
body and soul. Underneath my smoky breath, I muttered a litany
of winter woes.

For some inexplicable reason, I looked up as we turned the
corner by the neighborhood school and noticed the trees along
the athletic field fence. They formed silvery silhouettes against a
cloudless azure sky. I noticed nests, hidden during leafy seasons,
tucked among the bare branches. The variety fascinated me:
squirrel nests suspended high up in oak and pecan trees, tidy little bird nests in pear and crepe myrtle, loose casual constructions
of twigs and grass nestled in cedar and sweet gum limbs.

A nest is a home, a dwelling built to receive the gift of life. It
is prepared from everyday scraps: twigs, grasses, mud, moss,
clay, decayed wood, feathers, paper, and a variety of ordinary
things. But it awaits a birthing, a miracle.

A home is a nest, I mused, after the walk, while I warmed up with a sweetened cup of steaming Earl Grey. When one faces limited mobility and serious health issues, surroundings become hugely important. We caregivers and our loved ones have no choice but to spend most of our time at home. Yet many of us lose energy and interest in our nest. Some days we are tired and overwhelmed by our dauntingly heavy load.

Bob and I have discussed what makes a house a home and how we hope our home will be a house of prayer. By that we are expressing the desire for our dwelling place to be a welcoming haven for God and others. Our nest is prepared from ordinary fragments, from bits and pieces of our lives: twigs of tension and challenge, straws of struggle and perseverance, dry grass of daily dyings and discouragement, mud of hubris and sinfulness, soft down of love and devotion, and bright yarn strings of humor and gratitude.

————————

Prayer: Jesus, you had no place to call home when you lived on earth. Come, Lord, and grant us the privilege of claiming our heart-nests as your home. Show us ways to deal with winter times when our spirits feel frozen. Guide us to build a home that awaits a birthing, an aliveness of love and devoted care for our loved ones and you. Amen.

52
Bless You

—∞∞—

Scripture Reading: Numbers 6:22-27

The Lord bless you and keep you.

Numbers 6:24

Some years ago, several friends and I were experiencing difficult days. Joan's best friend died suddenly. Marty was going through a divorce. Charlene's son was experimenting with drugs. And on it went. The sky seemed to be tumbling down. But we got through those tough times and became deeper, more compassionate people as a result.

Now we are decades older. A couple of spouses have died, and the others are ill. Our own health and financial issues challenge us as well. The sky is tumbling down again. Where can we discover meaning in these events? What difference can our lives make? Are our efforts futile? How long can we keep going?

The image of God that comforted me in former struggles surfaces again to provide consolation. It first came to me in the form of a visual love note from the heart of a caring Almighty Creator during a time of silent meditation. It goes like this:

A flock of birds lies on their backs with their little twiglike legs stiffened and sticking straight up in the air. Some animals have told them the world is a mess and about to be annihilated. The sky is going to fall and crush the life out of God's critters. The birds love God and God's creation. Their frail skinny legs might not be able to do much to keep the falling sky from crushing the life out of God's created order, but by golly they are trying the best they know how.

About that time, God comes by and asks the birds what they were doing on their backs with their legs up in the air. They explain their little twiglike legs might not be able to catch the falling sky and prevent the destruction of Creation, but they are doing the best they possibly can.

A faint smile forms on God's face. The Lord looks at them with loving eyes and says, "My silly little birds, I see you are doing the best you possibly can and I would like to say . . ."

There is a long pause and the birds together say, "You would like to say . . . ?"

And God, in a rather shy embarrassed manner says, "I would like to say, *God bless you!*"

Are blessings important today, or were they something for Old Testament times? Our emotional and psychological makeup is such that we all need what the Bible calls "the blessing." Over the years, my short imaginative story has offered me comfort and encouragement. For all people caring for an impaired or chronically ill person, who sometimes feel their efforts can't make a difference but do the best they can anyhow, I would like to say, *"God bless you!"*

Prayer: Lord God, our hearts overflow with gratitude for the gift of your blessing. May we remember to share it with others. Amen.

Tears and Laughter

Blessed are you who weep now,
for you will laugh.

Luke 6:21b

53
Confused

~oo~

Scripture Reading: Mark 5:1-20

Then people came to see what it was that had happened. They came to Jesus and saw the demoniac sitting there, clothed and in his right mind.

Mark 5:14b-15a

"Nell, do you want me to put the trash out?"
"No, there's no trash pickup today. This is Sunday."

"Nell, I'm looking for my toast to put the jelly on."
"Bob, you've eaten your toast."

"Nell, what is that disease I have?"
"Are you trying to remember *diabetes*? You have that and others."

This kind of confusion frequently plagues Bob. What's so frustrating for me is that I can't figure out what it's about, and therefore I cannot do anything. I ask the doctor for answers, and he schedules another MRI test. Experience has proven Bob can come through one of those tests with normal results and experience a grand mal seizure a week later. I have lost faith in most tests and lab work. I live with my husband's confusion, and I know many of his responses are not normal. I feel like a spectator in a hopeless situation. I yearn for the mystery to be solved so we can find the road back home.

Bob came into the room where I was seated at the computer. "Nell, you are always writing. Want an idea for a story? You should write about a lost child; only the lost child is an adult who is lost and can't get out of where he is. He can't get out because we don't know where we are." Bob never even realized that he had shifted from third to first person. Those words spoke volumes to me about his confusion and disorientation. I cried.

Bob's illnesses have taken a toll on us both. My aversion and resistance to the changes often create unnecessary suffering. I need to learn to release everything to God because I can't make it okay.

Like the demoniac in today's scripture, we can be healed and regain our right mind by contact with a Lord who longs to set us free. It's time to get back on my knees and lay my problems on God's shoulders. God can calm my chaotic thoughts named Legion, send them into a herd of pigs, and rush those pigs down a steep bank to drown in the sea. God is like that, you know. God has a quirky sense of humor.

Prayer: Laughing Jesus, somehow when we hang out with you, life seems calm and happy. Within the light of your healing love, we don't need to know where we are because we are lost no longer. Amen.

54
Fleet Manager

Scripture Reading: Jude 1:20-21, 24-25

*To the only God our Savior, through Jesus Christ our Lord,
be glory, majesty, power, and authority, before all time and
now and forever. Amen.*

Jude 1:25

Bob's wheelchair obsession started nine years ago and shows no signs of ending. It began when he saw a newspaper ad for non-motorized wheelchairs being sold at a hardware store twenty miles away. He talked about how helpful one would be since he was having trouble walking. I finally agreed to drive him to the store to check them out, and he bought one on the spot. That was Wheelchair Number 1.

A month later Bob started talking about how nice it would be to have a motorized chair so I would not have to push him. He spoke with his doctor, who agreed it was a good idea. Bob located a dealership and persuaded me to drive him twenty-five miles to "shop." He chose a bright red, heavy-duty chair and some aluminum ramps for loading the thing in the back of our SUV. Bob now owned Wheelchair Number 2.

A neighbor's wife died, and my husband admired her smaller wheelchair stored in the garage. Negotiations took a year, with Bob eventually buying Wheelchair Number 3. I could not believe it. We don't have money to throw around, and he certainly did not need a third wheelchair. Besides, we now had a lift for loading, and this "new" chair was not outfitted for lift use. Bob had to call a grandson with a pick-up truck to get the chair and deposit it in our garage, where it remains unused.

Next Bob decided his old heavy red chair needed an overhaul. During phone discussions with the shop owner, he learned a replacement chair cost less than the repairs. Bob qualified for a new chair through Medicare, and his doctor faxed the required forms to the dealer.

I was appalled when shiny blue Wheelchair Number 4 arrived. Weeks of phone negotiations have resulted in a new loading system and repairs to Number 3.

Bob received numerous awards as a top national Chevrolet salesman. He sold thousands of police cars and vehicles of all kinds throughout North Texas. Our daughter and I chuckle about the wheelchairs. Now that he has amassed his fleet, he is scheming about what and how to sell. The fleet manager is alive and busy—with many battery packs to keep charged.

I too require a battery recharge regularly. Caregiving drains me, but I have at least learned where to find the source of all I need. Power is found when I go to God on my knees.

———————

Prayer: Eternal God, preserve us with your mighty power so we may not fall into sin nor be overcome by adversity. Give us patience when we have to deal with unusual situations like a fleet of wheelchairs and its manager. Amen.

55

Best-Ever Day

⸺ ∞ ⸺

Scripture Reading: Psalm 104:1-13

You [God] make springs gush forth in the valleys;
they flow between the hills.

Psalm 104:10

As soon as the kitchen is tidy after breakfast and my husband is settled, I rush to the guest room and snuggle into a comfortable armchair, appropriately called Grandma's Prayer Chair. For the next thirty or more minutes I enjoy reading, praying, and meditating. A favorite resource for this quiet time is *Daily Guideposts*, which my cousins send me for Christmas every year. I value it so much that I now give copies to twenty family and friends on my Christmas list.

One devotional I read this week told about a four-year-old girl's afternoon at the park, complete with treats from the ice cream truck. The attention she longed for and received that day from an older sister led the child to proclaim, "This was my best-ever day." I read those words and began to wonder about my own "best-ever day."

For months, my close friend and soul sister, Emily, and I planned to attend a writers' conference in Oklahoma City. The week before we were to go, the friend who had agreed to stay with my husband became so ill that he required blood transfusions, numerous tests, and a five-day hospitalization. Without a respite in eight months, I felt desperate for a break and helplessly snared in the caregiver's trap.

I frantically searched my files for information about some sitter businesses collected at an Alzheimer's symposium. I found the business cards, prayed, and then phoned. The interview and evaluation were arranged, I worked out details, and I went forward with my plans. En route to Emily's house, my elation caused me to break out singing the Doxology.

As planned, Emily and I stopped to hike at Turner Falls Park, a few miles north of the Red River across the Texas border in Oklahoma. The weather was perfect—crisp, sunny, and mild. Many sulfur springs from the Arbuckle Mountains form Honey Creek, which cascades in a seventy-seven-foot waterfall to a natural swimming pool called the Blue Hole. The sound of rushing water, birdcalls, and rustling leaves sent my heart into ecstasy.

Erosion has exposed geological formations of layers of granite and sedimentary strata uplifted some three hundred million years ago. I took in deep breaths and marveled at God's handiwork while studying these windows into the past rising on either side of the canyon where we hiked. I savored every joy-filled moment of my "best-ever day," a day that touched me to the core and refreshed my soul.

Prayer: Awesome Creator God, you made springs of water cascade between the mountains and rush to flood my heart with re-creation and gladness. I lift up my voice and sing praises to my Maker from whom all blessings flow. Amen.

56
The Numismatist

———

Scripture Reading: Matthew 22:15-22

But Jesus, aware of their malice, said,
"Why are you putting me to the test, you hypocrites?
Show me the coin used for the tax."

Matthew 22:18-19a

Bob has collected coins since he was seven years old, although he refuses to call himself a collector. He refers to his hobby as "accumulating coins," because he is an amateur who acquires only what he likes. Coin boxes are stacked inside and under his giant roll-top desk, on and under his office table, in his closet, and atop two small tables. The enormous, impressive collection continues to grow.

For several years Bob could not enjoy his hobby because of his illnesses and poor eyesight. Months passed after a life-threatening episode with a seizure and strokes before he could handle basic needs for himself. He was immobile and couldn't see. Depression and anxiety became formidable foes. I watched and prayed.

When Bob improved, I decided to give him the latest coin books and a membership in the Fort Worth Coin Club for Christmas. We began to attend meetings, and slowly Bob became interested in his hobby again. I am thankful for surgeries and a magnifying light that have enabled him to study, grade, and enjoy his coins. He spends hours happily engrossed in his hobby. He can't walk or do much else, but what joy Bob finds in being a numismatist (student of coins).

You do not have to be a coin enthusiast to appreciate this prayer poem by Charlotte van Stolk. I clipped it from a 1989 issue of *The Living Church* because it was so poignant and clever.

I am a coin, Gamble on me,
You gambling God.
Spinning my nickel soul across
life toward Your Kingdom's till.
What chance have I to make it,
see me wobble?

And when I fall flat
my name on both sides is Caesar's
for all to see.
Not Yours.

I spent myself
for bread
for vengeance for fun
for sin
They cost all I am and then some.
So now I'm not worth a nickel,
but less.

So why should You still care?
Is it because of Divine Patience
and somewhere
in the cosmic imagination
I precisely fit one slot
in the machinery of Your Power
and Glory that is
waiting for me? Amen.

Prayer: Thank you, Lord, for hobbies that provide entertainment and sense of purpose. May we all be good stewards who find a perfect fit in your Glorious Imagination. Amen.

57
June Bug

———◦◦◦———

Scripture Reading: Ephesians 3:7-12

In him and through faith in him we may approach God with freedom and confidence.

Ephesians 3:12, NIV

Same ol' daily daily-ness is draining my enthusiasm for being alive. The routine goes something like this: cook three meals, wash clothes, clean up, drive Bob to doctor appointments and rehab, dole out meds, check e-mails, take care of business, let the dog in, let the dog out. My personhood, my uniqueness, and my intellect are turning to mush.

Every week we go to a place that shatters the drudgery and rejuvenates my soul. Although it requires a huge effort to attend an early Sunday morning church service, we're always present, sitting at the back in a space provided for the large motorized wheelchair. Bob snoozes through most of the service, but he has a strong sense of the importance of worship with his church family. I am always nourished by something: the music, the prayers, the words, the bread, the people.

Tucked away in last week's sermon was the following story:

The commencement address speaker at a large university last spring concluded his remarks by telling the graduates and their families he had watched a little June bug while he was giving his talk. The June bug was down inside one of the lights at the front of the stage. It slowly climbed up the metal cylinder and got almost to the rim when it lost its footing and slid all the way back down. Again and again the bug climbed up to the rim, only to slide back to its starting point. The speaker said, "Isn't it tragic, that little June bug forgot it has wings? Graduates, please remember you can fly."

Like that small mahogany-colored scarab beetle, I have choices. I can live an earthbound existence of cares, sloth, worries, depression, and limiting behavioral patterns. Or I can choose a risen life of beauty, holiness, joy, peace, and love.

———————

Prayer: Creator God, you made us with an ability to choose our responses and attitudes about the circumstances we live in day by day. Grant us silly little June bugs hope-filled courage to lift our wings and fly into the radiating warmth of a glad, free, risen life. Amen.

58
Independence Day

Happy is the nation whose God is the LORD,
the people whom he has chosen as his heritage.

Psalm 33:12

This is the first time in twelve years I missed my hometown's old-fashioned Fourth of July parade. We attended even after Bob needed a wheelchair for mobility. Wearing red, white, and blue clothing and carrying a small cooler of soft drinks, we joined the crowds lining the parade route. I became quite proficient at situating the motorized chair for maximum viewing of floats, antique cars, clowns, marching bands, color guards, and other units.

The veterans in their too-tight uniforms—many amputees and wheelchair-bound—always evoked tears. My father served in World War II aboard a destroyer in the Pacific arena. My children's father served as a carrier pilot in the Vietnam War, and many of his comrades lost their lives. The first person taken prisoner in Vietnam was our neighbor on the base. I know firsthand the challenges of military life and the heavy costs and sacrifice for both personnel and their families.

Last year Bob didn't feel well, so I went to the parade alone. It was not the same, so this year I opted to stay home. After a long walk with the dog, I sat on the patio with a large mug of coffee, thinking about my country.

My years as a caregiver have led me to this puzzlement: how to keep a balance between the individual and being a part of something bigger than myself such as a marriage; how to manage being separate but joined and not lose sight of either my separateness or our togetherness. That kind of balance is needed in a family and also in a democracy. We live with a fundamental contradiction in the United States of America—the optimistic notion that there can be a union of individuals in which every person is king.

The teeter-totter seems to have tipped to the side of individualism. Materialism, me-ism, gluttony, and hedonism have crept into American culture. I wish we Americans were more like the ancient Hebrews, who understood themselves as a covenant people, bound together by their love for God and others.

Tonight Bob and I watched *A Capital Fourth* on PBS. I cried when the veterans came on the screen. They served for the individual rights and freedoms of others. God bless them and their families.

Prayer: Sovereign God, turn my people into a model of compassion connected to one another and the world. Reform America where she is out of balance and absorbed with self. Amen.

59
Ole Meanie

Scripture Reading: Psalm 100

Know that the LORD is God.
It is he that made us, and we are his;
we are his people, and the sheep of his pasture.

Psalm 100:3

"Y ou are not like you used to be. You were so sweet and kind. Now you've turned into an ole meanie."

My husband is right. I am not the same person I was before my identity changed to caregiver. Accused of being overly polite and sickeningly nice, heaven forbid this little gentlewoman should hurt anyone's feelings. Not only carefully taught to be a sweet Southern lady, I had been carefully taught to be a sweet *Christian* Southern lady.

Change can be ugly and unpleasant, but it doesn't necessarily follow that the change is unhealthy. I used to wait on Bob hand and foot, hovering over him to meet his every whim and need. At times he required that kind of assistance, but his health has improved dramatically this past year, and I occasionally tell him he can do for himself. I shout from my desk where I'm writing, "Bob, there is no reason why you can't get up from your recliner and get a Coke for yourself. It's time to get unspoiled and help me out a bit. You need to be doing your part now that you're better."

Granted, I may be going too fast too soon in this metamorphosis from sweet magnolia to steel magnolia, but I can't seem to help myself. I have learned to get up and ask medical professionals for what we need. No longer hesitant and demure, the CEO of this household gets the job accomplished without fluff and frills. There is no time for (nor merit to) lies, mendacity, or silliness when you are taking care of someone who is chronically ill. Unfortunately, or fortunately, the businesslike approach is making a menacing assault on my gentility.

Admittedly, sometimes, I am bluntly mean. At breakfast, I glared at my husband, but he didn't get the message. Finally, in a thoroughly hacked-off tone, I said, "Bob, you awakened without greeting me and started right in about how you have a sore throat today. Now you talk on and on about the color of your urine. I know you are sick, but for God's sake give me a break."

"Wow, what ticked you off? You aren't as nice as you used to be."

Right then I really felt nasty. I entertained downright evil thoughts and stomped off to pray.

———————

Prayer: Good Shepherd, I feel lost in this caregiving lifestyle, unable to find my way back home. We are your people and the silly sheep of your pasture, and yet you have promised to search until you've found us. Find us, Lord, and carry us safely home in your bosom where meanness and sweetness are not the criteria for belonging. Only Love counts. Amen.

60
Tea and Cookies

Scripture Reading: 1 Timothy 6:17-19

They are to do good, to be rich in good works, generous,
and ready to share.

1 Timothy 6:18

A story I read recently impressed me. I will retell it in my words.

A very proper lady went into a teashop and sat down at a table for two near a window. She ordered a pot of tea and prepared to eat a package of cookies she had in her purse. The woman pulled out her book and began to read.

The shop became crowded. A man sat down in the empty chair at the woman's table and also ordered a pot of tea. The lady looked up from her book long enough to notice he was quite thin and had Jamaican dreadlocks. She quickly returned to her book without acknowledging his presence. As she read, she reached down and took a cookie. She noticed the man did likewise. This upset her, but she ignored it and continued to read. After a while she took another cookie and so did he. This unnerved her, and she glared.

While she fumed silently, the man took the fifth and final cookie, broke it in half and offered it to her. She rose quickly, paid her money, and scurried out of the teashop.

The woman was enraged at the rudeness and presumption of the strange man. She got to her car and reached into her purse, fumbling for the car keys. There, to her distress, she discovered her package of cookies unopened.

I understand feelings of indignation and resentment when someone messes with my space, time, and stuff. Too many times I treat my poor husband like a child and speak to him with scolding words.

I also have times to "swallow crow," like today. My husband has difficulty with memory. He constantly interrupts me with requests to find something he has misplaced. This morning he wanted a business card and phone number for a wheelchair store. Wheelchairs are a sore subject with me, especially since Bob has purchased four.

With stirred emotions, I continued my insistent retort, "I don't have your business card." A few minutes went by. I've been wrong enough times that I searched my purse anyway. Then I went to a little business card box on my desk. There was Bob's card.

Prayer: Loving Lord, help us be less hasty to judge others. We care providers face a multitude of challenges daily. Please, Lord, give us generous, accepting, sharing hearts. Amen.

61
Sweet Smell of Death

Scripture Reading: 2 Corinthians 2:14-17

For we are the aroma of Christ to God among those who are being saved and among those who are perishing, to the one a fragrance from death to death, to the other a fragrance from life to life.

2 Corinthians 2:15-16a

"Nell, I'm dying."

I deposited the armload of clothes from the dryer on the bed and hurried to the recliner where Bob sat, eyes closed and legs outstretched.

"Bob, did I hear you say you are dying?"

"Yes, I am."

"What makes you think so?"

"I have the sweet smell of death all around me. It never goes away. I feel sick and nauseated, like I am dying."

I had never heard of the sweet smell of death. Bob looked fine to me, but he talked about it constantly. Obviously, he was worried, so I scheduled a visit to the internist the next morning. After a thorough checkup and a long conversation, the doctor concluded Bob's condition remained unchanged. Bob disagreed because of the relentless fragrance.

I kept a watchful eye on him and woke several times during the night to check on him. The next morning, I again carried clean clothes from the dryer to the bed. I was folding towels when it struck me. I went to the laundry room, got a dryer sheet, and took it to Bob to smell. "Is this the sweet smell of death?"

"Yes, that's it."

"Bob, I picked up a box of these sheets with a fragrance by mistake. I have always used the scent-free kind. These with the fragrance are going in the trash. I'll go to the store and get ones without the smell."

"Good."

Bob did not laugh, but my support group got a chuckle out of the story. We know how sensitive our patients are and how upsetting any small change can be to them.

In today's scripture, Paul's imagery of a triumphal procession may allude to the ancient idea of fragrance, used in victory marches or sacrificial events, as a sign of the presence of God or of divine wisdom. "The fragrance that comes from knowing him [Christ]" refers to Jesus as the wisdom of God, not only preached but also manifested in his ministers.

Verses 15 and 16 also typify those multilayered contrasts that Paul loves. "Death to death" may be a phrase to describe persons who are living without the knowledge of Christ and are headed toward an ultimate end. "Life to life" refers to an authentic existence with Christ that leads to eternal life. Unabashedly, Bob and I choose life. No more "sweet smell of death."

Prayer: Fill us with knowledge of you, dear God, so we may be used as a sweet incense of your divine presence to those in our care. Amen.

62
A Bad Sad

—∞∞∞—

Scripture Reading: Psalm 77:1-10

I cry aloud to God,
aloud to God, that he may hear me.
In the day of my trouble I seek the Lord.

Psalm 77:1-2a

After signing in my husband at the doctor's reception desk, I sat next to his wheelchair and pulled out my knitting. Bob closed his eyes for a snooze. An elderly lady with lively eyes took the empty chair next to me and immediately asked what I was making. I reached in my bag and pulled out two completed Preemie caps while explaining that a group from my church makes items for a large charity hospital. She made a fist with one hand and adorned it with a tiny pink cap. She studied her "hand baby" silently for a minute and then told me she had never been able to have children.

"That must have been difficult for you and your husband."

Annie quickly responded, "Yes, it was a bad sad for a long time, but my husband's work sent him all over the world, and I got to travel around with him. That would've been hard on children."

The petite woman told me her husband died four years ago. "I am thankful for the sixty years we had together, but I still miss him. We married Thanksgiving weekend, and this time of year is hard. I get a bad sad during the holidays."

I learned Annie would be eighty-eight the following month and would have Thanksgiving dinner with a neighbor on her "street of angels." She told me about the difficulty of living on a fixed income but expressed gratitude for her good health and her strong faith. The conversation ended when Bob was called back to the doctor's examining room.

Thanksgiving is a feast instituted only after the pilgrims endured difficult living conditions and great hardships. The early observance was not a time of trinkets and trifles and Macy's parades but a recognition of the preciousness of survival. Annie seemed to have cultivated the virtue of thankfulness in spite of, and perhaps because of, her "bad sad" life experiences. She labeled her years caring for a sick husband "a blessing."

My encounter with Annie led me to remember Jesus' focus on the goodness and aliveness of God even in his most gruesome hours of passion and death. From the cross he neither judged nor condemned nor cast out. He alerted us to a new way of existence that embraces good, bad, sad, and glad while preparing us to patiently live fully for the duration of our lives. His Shepherd's heart stretches beyond paradox and teaches us God is present in every part of our lives.

God, Immanuel, is here with us through it all. Now that's reason for a Thanksgiving banquet. Pass the pumpkin pie, please.

———————

Prayer: Dear God, thank you, thank you, thank you. Amen.

63

Sweatshirts and Sweat

———— ∞∞∞ ————

Scripture Reading: Genesis 3:17-19; Luke 22:44

By the sweat of your brow
you will eat your food
until you return to the ground.

Genesis 3:19a, NIV

One of the discomforts that surprised me as a caregiver is the thermostat war. Our home is like an oven 24/7, every month, season, and year. My husband's illnesses have affected his body's ability to maintain normal temperature.

On the other hand, my mostly healthy body is functioning on energy-efficient settings. I am miserable with the house at 78 to 80 degrees, unless I'm sitting under a ceiling fan operating at high speed. I complain; Bob complains. I turn the thermostat down; Bob turns it up. He sits around in his sweatshirts; I sit around in my sweat.

Today's breakfast conversation went like this:

"I'm burning up in this house," I said, wiping my brow and fanning myself with the newspaper.

"If you start turning the heat down again, I'll shoot your fingers off."

"That's terrible, Bob, what a mean thing to say."

"Then don't turn the heat down," my husband retorted, while making a gesture with a pointed finger like shooting a pistol and then blowing the smoke from the end of its barrel. I think a smile almost broke through his dead-serious expression, but I did not stick around. I quickly grabbed up empty cereal bowls and headed for the kitchen, where I burst into laughter. I think he communicated quite effectively; he is still a mighty force to be reckoned with. He cannot control what is happening to his body and mind, but he can control the thermostat.

For the fun of it, I thought I would check the concordance to see if "sweat" appears in the Bible and discovered two references. The third chapter of Genesis records the disobedience and fall of Adam and Eve. The Lord God told Adam and Eve and the serpent the consequences for breaking their relationship with God. Adam would sweat, strain, and toil to put food on his family's table the rest of his earthly days. Eve would sweat too fixing meals, even though the Lord God did not recognize her contribution.

The second reference is found in Luke 22:44. Following the Last Supper with his disciples, Jesus went up the southwestern slope of the Mount of Olives to an olive grove called Gethsemane. He prayed with such extreme anguish over what he faced that his sweat was like drops of blood.

Prayer: Jesus Christ, my Redeemer and Lord, you paid the greatest possible sacrifice of Love for our atonement. Help us to live patiently with beads of perspiration across our brow as a small sacramental reminder of what you have done for us. Amen.

64
The Gift of Laughter

Scripture Reading: Luke 6:17-21

Blessed are you who are hungry now,
for you will be filled.
Blessed are you who weep now,
for you will laugh.

Luke 6:21

My best friend (we call each other "soul sister") is the wonderfully creative, fun-loving baby of her family. She constantly reminds me to lighten up, then she proceeds to tell one of her jokes or something she finds humorous. Because I am a serious, super responsible, oldest child with five siblings, I need her perspective. Often I find myself saying, "Thanks, I needed that."

I have observed in support group meetings that at some point during the sharing of experiences and feelings a participant will relate a story that cracks us wide open with laughter. The laughs come from deep within, perhaps from a place down near our toes, bringing sacred relief from the pain, suffering, and sacrifice of our daily existence. Invariably someone will comment, "Thanks, I needed that."

At a recent meeting a group member told about finding pajamas in the refrigerator, and that triggered the sharing of several "funnies." A lovely, auburn-haired woman told us life improved when she found a geriatric doctor for her mother. The doctor begins every visit with a mini–mental exam: "What is your name? What is your date of birth? Where do you live? Who is the president?"

Janie continued, "We have been through this routine several times over the past two years. Last week Mother walked in, and without even waiting to greet the doctor began her spiel. "I am Beth Jones. My date of birth is February 21, 1924. I live in Bedford, Texas, and the president is George Bush. Now let's get on with it."

Laughter tumbled out like the sound of happy, babbling brooks splashing downstream to glad ocean waters. Gladness is not attained by avoidance of pain and suffering. In all situations joy and humor give power to rise above sorrow. I have a sneaking suspicion laughter may be the private language of heaven. Today we laughed, and God laughed too.

Prayer: Thank you, wise and compassionate God, for the gift of laughter. What an ingenious technique you created to meet our needs. Joy does not exclude hardship and suffering, but it offers hope and balm to what pains the soul. As the younger generation would say, "Cool." Amen.

65
Angels

Scripture Reading: Matthew 28:1-10

Suddenly there was a great earthquake; for an angel of the Lord, descending from heaven, came and rolled back the stone and sat on it.

Matthew 28:2

Annually, three weeks before Christmas, I take a box of carefully wrapped angels from the attic. Each winged creation was a gift, and I recall the giver while I unwrap and set up the angel display. The ritual delights my inner child and helps prepare my heart and hearth to receive the Christ child anew.

Every angel is my favorite, but one is my favorite favorite. She lives outside the box year-round on the piano. Sculpted with laser technology inside a two-by-three-inch crystal cube, she rests on a black carved wooden stand. She appears three-dimensional with flowing robe and gossamer wings. A few stars surround her as she blows her trumpet to herald the good news. How someone could delineate something so exquisite, tiny, and detailed inside a block of crystal boggles my mind.

The moment when I received my cube angel thrilled me. Bob no longer drives since his last seizure, so I drove him to an appointment with his neurologist a few days before Christmas 2004. When he checked in, the receptionist handed him a pretty gift bag. He turned and handed it to me, saying, "You are my angel, and I would not be alive if it were not for you. Happy

Christmas!" I stammered and blubbered, while he and Holly enjoyed the fruits of their collaboration to surprise me.

Today I sat at the piano and glanced over at my crystal angel. I recalled some scripture passages about angels. Angel appearances in the Bible intrigue and draw me into the mysteriousness of God. In Luke angels announce the birth of the Bethlehem Babe to the shepherds. In the book of Revelation the symbolic imagery of seven angels blowing on seven trumpets signals God's activity during the apocalyptic days of prophetic revelation.

The angel in Matthew's version of the Resurrection puzzles and amuses me. Matthew reports: "Suddenly there was a great earthquake; for an angel of the Lord, descending from heaven, came and rolled back the stone and sat on it." I can picture it. The angel performed this amazing feat and then casually climbed up on the stone. God must have a sense of humor. Something so bizarre and wildly miraculous happened, and the angel simply sat there with his legs crossed while the women gasped. What a surprising way to show victory over death!

Prayer: Dear God, special acts of love from family and friends are a joy. Teach each of us care providers how to be an authentic earth angel for our beloved. Amen.

66

Attitude Is Everything

—◦◦◦—

Scripture Reading: 1 Samuel 17:41-51

David said to the Philistine, "You come to me with sword and spear and javelin; but I come to you in the name of the Lord of hosts . . . whom you have defied."

1 Samuel 17:45

The day was blah—laundry, housekeeping, grocery shopping, cooking, drawing up another week's supply of meds. But later, when I checked my e-mail, I got a chuckle out of what I found.

The sender of this and many e-mails over the past year causes me to smile with her marvelous, positive attitude. Ada always greets me, "Hi, baby, how in the world are you?" As I near seventy, I find it amusing being called "baby." But in this case it is quite appropriate since Ada was a bridge buddy of my grandmother and mother eons ago. For decades she was an inspirational teacher who had a huge impact on kids in a small rural Mississippi town, my sister among them.

When Hurricane Katrina swept away Ada's lifetime of possessions, she moved in with her son and his wife here in Texas. We reconnected at church. Her enthusiasm for life, learning, and people enabled her to build friendships in her new home as well as nurture old ones via the Internet. This is the amusing story (by an anonymous author) she passed along to me:

There once was a woman who woke up one morning, looked in the mirror, and noticed she had only three hairs on her head. "Well," she said, "I think I'll braid my hair today." So she did and had a wonderful day.

The next day she woke up, looked in the mirror and saw she had only two hairs on her head. "Mmm," she said, "I think I'll part my hair down the middle today." So she did and had a grand day.

The next day she woke up, looked in the mirror and noticed she had only one hair on her head. "Well," she said, "today I'm going to wear my hair in a pony tail." So she did and had a fun, fun day.

The next day she woke up, looked in the mirror and noticed there wasn't a single hair on her head. "Yay!" she exclaimed, "I don't have to fix my hair today!"

Attitude is everything.

The young shepherd David believed he could defeat the gigantic Philistine Goliath because he had God on his side. His confidence, based on a profound trust in the Lord, empowered him to prevail with a sling and a stone. Belief in a steadfast, loving, merciful God fosters a positive attitude in all circumstances—caregiving, debilitating illness, nasty hurricanes, or warring neighbors.

———————

Prayer: Almighty God, when we face tough situations, you are with us. May our trust in your providence grow the kind of attitude that propels us to dance in the rain until the storms pass. Amen.

67
Bath Time

‐⸙‐

Scripture Reading: Luke 5:12-14

*Then Jesus stretched out his hand, touched him, and said,
"I do choose. Be made clean."*

Luke 5:13a

Problems often arise for caregivers directing impaired persons to change their clothes or take a bath. Sometimes the care receivers become depressed or apathetic, thereby losing any desire to bathe. Many have a fear of falling. Some find the business of bathing and dressing too complicated and confusing because these tasks require decision making and physical exertion.

Dressing and bathing are personal activities symbolic of basic independence, and having someone's eyes and hands on our naked, not-so-beautiful, aging bodies makes us uncomfortable. So the distress people feel certainly is understandable.

During the months when my husband received home health care, an aide came to help him with baths. We did what we could to respect his privacy by laying out everything he would need. We held up a bath sheet when he undressed and covered him while helping him in and out of his tub chair. But, despite all these efforts, he intensely disliked the situation.

One woman in our support group learned not to tell her mother she "needed" a bath. Mom associated "needed" with body odor. Disease had destroyed her sense of smell, and she knew she didn't smell bad. One woman tells her husband that after his bath, they will enjoy his favorite cookies. Generally the most effective formula is simply to tell care receivers their bath is ready and to talk them through the process step by step calmly.

A man in our group told us about the improvement a sliding bench made in moving his wife in and out of the tub. Others lauded the walk-in premium tubs, but the main drawback is their cost. Handheld showerheads are fantastic. One caregiver says she passes one to her husband after the bath and tells him to "play in the rain."

We laughed with a woman who told a story about her brother with dementia. His hearing aids were removed for his bath, to be administered by a home health care aide. The aide came in, took his vital signs, and then said, "Let's go get in your bath." Her brother thought she said, "Let's go get in your bed." He became irate and yelled for her to leave his house immediately. Although told what she really said, he refused to have anything more to do with outside helpers.

Our group heard another story from a woman whose husband had for many years routinely taken a shower after he mowed the lawn. He now has Alzheimer's disease, and a lawn service mows the lawn. As soon as the hired man finishes the yard work, her husband takes a shower.

Our bodies and minds may confuse and confound us, but, regardless, God's overflowing, unconditional love washes over us and makes us whole.

Prayer: Jesus, you healed the leper and made him clean. Touch us, Lord, and cleanse our hearts in order to receive you in the midst of our daily tasks. Wash our weariness with a little laughter. Amen.

68
Geniuses

—∞∞∞—

Scripture Reading: James 1:2-5

If any of you is lacking in wisdom, ask God, who gives to all generously and ungrudgingly, and it will be given you.

James 1:5

It happens every time I attend a caregivers support group session. The attendees are absolute geniuses. They educate, encourage, support, share, and love one another in ways that are the best of Christianity in action. I feel I am among people who took down the doors to their houses and opened their lives and their souls in complete hospitality. They have invited one another not only into their homes but also into their closets of trial, sadness, and hard-won wisdoms. The doors they removed have been laid out on sawhorses and turned into banquet tables where weary hearts find nourishment for their pilgrimage.

Personal stories bring tears and outbursts of spontaneous laughter. When asked how his wife was doing, a longtime member of the group replied, "This is the longest plateau ever. She goes on and on under hospice care at the nursing home. I go often to see her, but she is asleep or staring at the wall. Occasionally she will grab my finger, and I'm thrilled when that happens."

We inquired about another member's one-week respite. She cares for her mother with Alzheimer's disease and a sister with mental handicaps. Siblings and friends were filling in for her and apparently furnished a diet of fast food while she was away. Her

— 150 —

mother's comment upon Josie's return was, "I'm sure glad to have my cook back."

One member constantly amazes us with her almost childlike genius in handling her husband who is in middle-stage Alzheimer's. She described what happened when she took him to a restaurant recently. They got in the car to go, but when she turned on the ignition, he got out of the car and headed back into the house. She asked, "Where are you going? We're supposed to go to the restaurant now."

He responded, "I'm going back in the house to get my wife and tell her to come on."

Wife Mary wisely said, "Oh, didn't you know she's going to meet us there?"

The husband returned to the car and off they went. When they arrived at the restaurant, Mary said, "Now you go in first, and your wife will be along soon." She followed him in, got him seated, and left. When she returned, he looked up at her and calmly spoke, "Oh, there you are."

———————

Prayer: Holy Spirit, Fount of Wisdom, thank you for helping us to find knowledge, understanding, and joy in our trials through the encouragement and love of other caregivers. May those who do not have a support network locate one without delay. Amen.

69
Serendipity

—∞∞—

Scripture Reading: Mark 4:26-32

*[Jesus] also said, "The kingdom of God is as if someone
would scatter seed on the ground, and would sleep and
rise night and day, and the seed would sprout and grow,
he does not know how."*

Mark 4:26-27

My husband had a restless night, so letting him sleep later this morning was a no-brainer. I sat down to breakfast, enjoying the solitude and stillness. But the silence was soon filled with a rich *what-cheer, cheer, cheer, purty-purty-purty-purty* followed by metallic *chip-chip-chips*. I looked and saw a bright red male cardinal dipping into the lawn sprinkler spray and then hopping over to the bush next to the windowsill. He fluttered his wings, shook off water droplets, and repeated the pattern—into the sprinkler and back to the bush.

Several times the eight-inch feathery visitor turned his red-crested head with black face and stout reddish orange bill directly toward me. The song seemed to grow louder and more jubilant for his appreciative audience of one. The accomplished songster was singing in the shower, and he had granted me the privilege of sharing in his private watery joy. My reaction to this serendipitous gift was to sing along: "This is the day the Lord has made—*what-cheer, cheer, cheer*; let us rejoice and be glad in it—*purty-purty-purty-purty*."

My little red friend departed after his bath, but I knew he would return. A feeder nearby holds a special wild-bird mix containing large, oily black sunflower seeds, a cardinal favorite. Growing up around this feeder are other delightful surprises. Some of the seeds fell to the ground, sprouted, and grew into tall, green, leafy plants with large, yellow-rayed flower heads beginning to turn brown as seeds develop.

Bob and I marveled at the speed of their growth and the way the flowers' faces turn toward the sun. We did not plant nor expect the colorful display outside our window, and that is another cause for awe. But the biggest surprise and puzzle of all, for me, is how God managed to get such a big plant with a plate-size golden bloom into such a small black seed. The mysteries of a Creator who thought up cardinals and sunflowers evoke my wonder and praise.

Prayer: Lord God, Creator of the Universe, thank you for the unexpected gifts a morning can bring. The song of a red bird, yellow blossoms from unplanted seeds, or whatever serendipity of nature stirs our spirit and moves us to thanksgiving. We become more contented caregivers when we remember your miracles, especially the greatest one of all, your Son, Christ Jesus, whose Spirit assures all your children we are miracles too. Amen.

70

Big Spenders

—∞∞—

Scripture Reading: Mark 11:15-17

On reaching Jerusalem, Jesus entered the temple area and began driving out those who were buying and selling there.

Mark 11:15a

An impaired person can become irresponsible with money. Before seizures, strokes, and surgeries, my husband handled finances deftly. Then he began forgetting to pay bills, couldn't balance the checkbook, misplaced documents, and misread numbers.

The transfer of financial responsibilities to me hit some rocks in the road but few boulders. Bob has been surprisingly willing to take his hands off the reins, and I have managed somehow to keep the wagon between the ditches.

Difficulty with money matters is a topic that surfaces frequently at support group meetings. An attractive woman named Cora had a major problem with her husband's compulsive spending. He ordered the latest in expensive kitchen appliances plus a washer and a dryer without her knowledge. Their relatively new appliances certainly did not need to be replaced. But he had seen commercials on television about all the modern features and promptly used the credit card to make his purchases.

Cora discovered what he had done when the store called to arrange a delivery time. She cancelled the order. Sneaky Pete ordered the appliances again. This time Cora managed to cancel the order a second time except for an expensive refrigerator.

Now Pete studies catalogs and places orders when he goes to his office several times a week, even though he is no longer working. Cora complained she spends a small fortune on postage returning his catalog purchases. She cancelled the credit card, but Pete applied for another one. This dear woman is living a nightmare.

Cora's problem is not one I have faced, but apparently others have. Gloria told about her mother's compulsive shopping for linens, especially bath towels. Mom purchased huge stacks of items, and Gloria came along and returned them to the store a few days later. The mother is now in a nursing home, so the shopping sprees have ended.

Gloria chuckled, "Linens were not Mother's only compulsion. After we moved her to the nursing home, I found twelve cartons of Cool Whip in the fridge."

The questions arose: What can I do? What should I tolerate? Where do I set boundaries? It's not possible to rationalize with Alzheimer's patients and people with mental impairments, mild or severe. More often than not, we must "roll with it" and become deviously clever at finding ways to offset the care receiver's behavior without their knowing. Taking that route can preserve peace and save the dignity of our "big spenders."

Prayer: Lord God, teach us to be good stewards of our finances. Amen.

71
Pity Party

─ ∞∞∞ ─

Scripture Reading: Psalm 88

Let my prayer come before you;
incline your ear to my cry.

Psalm 88:2

The psalms fall into categories: mad, glad, and sad. The sad ones remind me of many country songs with their honest and authentic expression of life experiences. I feel sad today, so I chose the saddest psalm of the 150 for today's reading. I am tired of being stoic and putting on a fake smiley face for family and friends. I want to wallow in self-pity today.

One promise I made myself when I began writing these devotionals was to be honest, candid, and authentic. Many beautiful Christian disciples might scold and ask, "Where is your faith?" I can hear them now: "The very idea of throwing a pity party. You *should* have the joy of the Lord. Adjust your attitude and get over it."

Maybe later today, or tomorrow, I will follow their advice, but for now, like the miserable psalmist, I cry unto the Lord. I am hosting a real pity party. The tears are the first I have allowed myself in a long, long time.

My mind often works in unpredictable ways. I just thought about an old song, popular in the 1960s, titled "It's My Party." Singer-songwriter Lesley Gore wrote the song when she was sixteen. The lyrics tell the story of losing a boyfriend to another girl in the course of a birthday party, which should have been a happy occasion. She justifies her inevitable response in the chorus: "It's my party and I'll cry if I want to."

My husband is not the same man I married. We no longer dance, go to ballgames and movies, travel, or enjoy intimate evenings. Bob was exceptionally dynamic, witty, and fun. He still is an incredible man, but being his caregiver is not the same as being his marriage partner. Sometimes I miss the old lover. And "I'll cry if I want to."

———————

Prayer: Compassionate Lord of the Universe, thank you for the gift of tears. They wash away our sadness and bring therapeutic relief to our daily existence. Perhaps there is a tiny tear from heaven to mingle with ours. Amen.

72
Acorns and Pumpkins

—⟨∞⟩—

Scripture Reading: Psalm 104:24, 27-33

These [your creatures] all look to you
to give them their food in due season;
when you give to them, they gather it up;
when you open your hand,
they are filled with good things.

Psalm 104:27-28

My favorite month is October. The sky is the bluest, the air turns crisp, and the harvest season gets into full swing. Apples, gourds, pumpkins, acorns, sunflowers, scarecrows, and multicolored leaves evoke a sense of well-being and vitality that is hard to explain. I switch out clothes and change up our cuisine. I find recipes for rich soups, chili, and thick substantial breads. The time has returned for gingerbread with lemon sauce, creamy pumpkin pie, fresh apple cake with caramel sauce, and pears poached in sweet wine.

During my first two caregiving years, I was depressed and bewildered. I didn't care about autumn, Christmas, or much of anything. But the fog has lifted, and this year my old excitement for fall has returned. I have decorated grapevine wreaths with welcoming leaves, berries, and sunflowers—one over the mantel, another by the front door. Pumpkins sit by a garden bench on the front lawn and by a barrel of dried grasses and assorted foliage at the doorway. Two small pumpkins rest on the hearth next to an old crock full of sunflowers.

An arrangement of dried leaves, acorns, and spice-scented candles adorns the dining room table, which has been covered with a cheerful autumn-themed tablecloth. Yes, it is fall festive around here. Bob and I are mostly confined to home now—all the more reason the house needs to look perky and happy. I did it for us. Caregivers and care receivers merit and appreciate pleasant surroundings.

Autumn brings to mind an anonymous poem about a woman walking through a meadow, admiring the wonders of nature. A majestic oak tree stood in the corner of a field of plump orange pumpkins. The woman walked over and sat down under the tree. She observed that tiny acorns grew on huge branches and huge pumpkins on tiny vines. She thought, "God blundered with Creation! He should have put the small acorns on the tiny vines and the large pumpkins on the huge branches."

Growing sleepy, the woman stretched out to take a nap. A few minutes after falling asleep, she was awakened by a tiny acorn bouncing off her nose. She chuckled as she rubbed her nose and spoke to herself, "Maybe God had it right after all!"

———————

Prayer: God of Seasons, we are in the autumn of our lives. We have challenges and trials, but we trust you to know what is best for us. Troubles the size of acorns are far better than falling pumpkins any season of the year. Amen.

73
A Godly Grief

Scripture Reading: 2 Corinthians 7:8-13a

*For godly grief produces a repentance that leads to salvation
and brings no regret, but worldly grief produces death.*

2 Corinthians 7:10

After Paul established the church at Corinth, he carried on an extensive correspondence with the Christians there. They wrote him at least once, and he wrote them a minimum of four times. Today's reading, found in 2 Corinthians, expresses the author's delight at the church's penitent response to his previous, tearful, scolding letter. The Corinthian Christians rejoined their hearts to God in "godly grief" rather than pursuing a worldly bereavement built on resentment.

The subject of grief came up several times during an Alzheimer's support group meeting. A facilitator asked Jolene how she'd been since the last session. She answered, voice filled with strong emotion, "Things have been horrible."

The facilitator asked, "What do you mean by *horrible*?"

Jolene explained that one weekend her husband suddenly couldn't walk. When he became belligerent and impossible to handle physically, she called 911. The ambulance took Tom to a nearby hospital ER, where he had to be forcibly restrained. This upset him even more. Because hospital staff was too limited at night to handle the special needs of an Alzheimer's patient,

Jolene hired a nurse to watch her husband from 7:00 in the evening until 7:00 the next morning when she returned.

A few days later the hospital discharged Tom and assigned him to a rehab facility. Under Medicare, he's permitted to stay up to one hundred days, with the proviso he demonstrates progress. Unfortunately, this type of care is inadequate since Alzheimer's patients don't fit in with the general population. For instance, during a difficult "sundowner" (late-afternoon fit), Tom attacked a nurse's aide, pinning her arms behind her back. Jolene described how horrified she was to witness such radical changes in her once-gentle husband.

After the episode, Jolene had to face the fact that she could no longer keep her husband at home. None of the established facilities had openings. Her continued search led her to a new center, but she would have to drive thirty minutes each way to visit. She decided to place him there despite the inconvenient commute, because she believed this facility would treat her husband with respect.

The group, upon hearing her tale, expressed approval of her difficult decisions in caring for her husband. Several nodded when Jolene closed her report with these words: "We think it is all over when we put them in a care facility, but it's not. I cry all the way home after every visit. The house is so empty. I'll grieve for the rest of my life."

As caregivers, we must keep an eye on the nature of our sorrows. Jolene, like many caregivers, is in the process of experiencing godly grief and shifting burdens to shoulders designed to carry them.

Prayer: Lord God, hear our prayer as we come to you in need of support during our times of loneliness and grief. May we find divine comfort in the shelter of your merciful love. Amen.

74
Cat in the Hat Comes Back

⸺⊗⊗⊗⸺

Scripture Reading: Nehemiah 8:9-12

Do not be grieved, for the joy of the LORD is your strength.
Nehemiah 8:10

My local chapter of the Society of Children's Book Writers & Illustrators (SCBWI) was hosting a conference. I decided to support the project with my attendance and work as a volunteer. As a retired children's librarian and caregiver for my husband, I thought writing for children would be a great outlet for me. So I joined the organization.

Friday afternoon I went to the hotel, performed my volunteer duties, hurried home to get Bob's meds and supper, and returned for the dinner and a costume party. I had borrowed my old costume from the library and went as "The Cat in the Hat." Some of my happiest hours as a librarian came during preschool and school visits as well as in time spent designing and presenting story hours. The kids loved "The Cat" and even the quiet, shy ones magically came to life when this notorious character appeared.

With blackened nose and large parentheses eyebrows for the SCBWI gala, I felt alive again. My immense joy burned away feelings of sadness and loss. Reluctantly I left the party early to rush home, where I found my husband safe in his recliner quietly watching television. What a relief!

The next morning I fixed meals and meds, set everything up for the day, and headed back to volunteer duties and workshops.

The conference was going great until I decided to call home before the awards luncheon. Bob did not answer the phone. I tried several more times, wolfed down lunch, then tried again. He finally answered and told me he felt really bad. I exited the hotel hastily, mumbling about missing the afternoon and closing events. I bade farewell to the joy that fleetingly had filled my creative spirit and renewed my dreams of writing. I wanted "The Cat in the Hat" mystique back.

Nothing serious was wrong with Bob. Mostly he felt lonely. Perhaps this was a subconscious manipulation to get me home.

I did, however, later find some joy reading the scripture lesson from Nehemiah. After the Babylonian exile and the restoration of the Temple, the priest-scribe Ezra gathered the Israelites together and read aloud from the Mosaic book of law. Then he said to them, "Do not be grieved, for the joy of the LORD is your strength."

———————

Prayer: Holy Father, I hear joy calling our name, pursuing us, stretching out arms to embrace us so tightly that no worldly cares can destroy the joy of the Lord that strengthens us—with or without a cat costume. Amen.

75
Rainbows

Scripture Reading: Genesis 9:8-17

When the bow is in the clouds, I will see it and remember the everlasting covenant between God and every living creature of all flesh that is on the earth.

Genesis 9:16

Sometimes patterns or themes emerge in my readings. It's as if the Spirit wants me to pay attention to specific words or ideas. This week I repeatedly bumped into rainbow words. The first incidence occurred when I picked up *Splinters in My Pride* by Marilee Zdenek, and the book fell open at a photograph of hills, valley, and turbulent sky. These lines appeared on the opposite page:

> All those times, before I found the
> sun, much less the
> rainbow, you stayed close and warmed my lonely
> spirit with your touch. Dear special friend —
> without you,
> how cold and black the
> darkness would have been.

I read the poem a second and third time. Stormy days have come, but so have friends with cards, food, phone calls, and prayers to offer us breaks in the thunderclouds. Through weeks, months, and years of Bob's complex health issues, caring people have been, and continue to be, our Special Jesus Friends. They not only remind us it won't rain forever but also point to colorful wonders forged from a mixture of sun and showers.

In my bookcase, next to the first book, was *Reaching for Rainbows* by Ann Weems. I found this poem expressing precisely how I feel about my relationship with Bob and his life of chronic pain.

> If I could, I'd write for you a rainbow
> And splash it with all the colors of God
> And hang it in the window of your being
> So that each new God's morning
> Your eyes would open first
> to Hope and Promise.
> If I could, I'd wipe away your tears
> And hold you close forever in shalom.
> But God never promised
> I could write a rainbow,
> Never promised I could suffer for you,
> Only promised I could love you.
> That I do.

Thirdly, my devotions led me to the story of the Great Flood in Genesis 6:5–9:17. God held an expectation for the world, but the people God created refused to be God's creation. The scripture depicts no angry tyrant God who sends the Flood but rather a troubled, anguished, heartbroken parent. Noah, a model of faith, not only survived but also received a blessing and a covenant. The rainbow promise belongs to humankind. Hear the good news: "it won't rain always"—because God loves.

———————

Prayer: Thank you, God of Hope, who loves to everlasting. In the darkest days we have to face, may we remember you have a rainbow heart. Amen.

76
Children's Sabbath

———ം⊗⊗ം———

Scripture Reading: Matthew 19:13-15

*Jesus said, "Let the little children come to me, and do not
stop them; for it is to such as these that the kingdom of
heaven belongs."*

Matthew 19:14

Many traditional churches are literally dying. Their congregations are older people. Bob and I are blessed to belong to a vibrant church with young couples, children, and teens. All the generations gather on Sundays and holy days to worship together. Some Sunday services spotlight one of the various groups or different programs. Today we focused on children and our ministries to them, both locally and worldwide.

The scripture verses for today's reading depict a lovely incident in the gospel story. The context for the episode is a society where children held the lowest social status of all people. They had few rights, little recognition, and no power. In a matter of minutes, Jesus turned their value in and to the world upside down. I truly believe this was one of the most significant acts Jesus did. He reached down and placed the weak, lowly, poor ones on his knee and blessed them. He fulfilled the divine message that God loves us, does not condemn us, wraps arms around us, laughs and plays with us, and transfers beneficence to *everyone*. The world's classifications and judgments are insignificant. What wonderful news that is for the vast majority of humanity!

The debilitated, the sick, the dying, and the people who care for them can find great comfort in this scene when Jesus tells the disciples to let the children come to him. I smile when I entertain the notion of Jesus taking Bob and me on his knee and tickling our bare feet. Perhaps our Lord shares a knock-knock joke with my joke-loving husband who clings to Jesus' back hoping for a piggy-back ride. No one is a nuisance or a bother to Jesus; no one is unimportant. The way to his presence remains open eternally to the humblest person and the youngest child.

As we grow older and deal with issues of aging and poor health, we often grow further from God rather than nearer. There would be no bigger tragedy than believing the cares, challenges, and heartaches we caregivers and care receivers face daily do not matter to God. They do. And so we sing a happy verse from "Tell Me the Stories of Jesus":

> First let me hear how the children stood round his
>   knee,
> and I shall fancy his blessing resting on me;
> words full of kindness, deeds full of grace,
> all in the lovelight of Jesus' face.

Prayer: Jesus, make us like children—simple, trusting, loving. Help us forsake arrogance and sophistication. Grant us childlike eyes to see wonder and beauty unfolding around us each day. Amen.

77

The Sanctuary Herd

Scripture Reading: Proverbs 18:24, 27:10

Some friends play at friendship
but a true friend sticks closer
than one's nearest kin.

Proverbs 18:24

In 1995 two former elephant trainers, Carol Buckley and Scott Blais, had seen so much neglect and abuse at circuses and zoos they were inspired to create a haven where elephants could live out their lives peacefully. They developed a 2,700-acre preserve in Hohenwald, Tennessee, now recognized as the largest natural-habitat sanctuary for pachyderms in the United States. Nineteen residents enjoy what Buckley considers the three staples for happiness: freedom from dominance, room to roam, and a community of others like themselves.

An animal rights activist arranged for one resident, Jenny, to be transferred from a dog-and-cat shelter. Jenny had been dumped there after suffering a crippling leg injury. In the circus, Jenny had often been crammed into small train cars traveling from city to city, or she was tied up for twenty-three hours a day. After arriving at the sanctuary, Jenny was kept alone in a yard for one day due to her injury. Isolation proved so stressful for her, she soon was released to join the herd. Something surprising happened.

Twenty-three years earlier, Jenny had met Shirley, who became a surrogate mother to the young calf. They toiled in the circus together but were separated a few weeks later. When Jenny joined the sanctuary herd, she immediately found Shirley. The two greeted each other by trumpeting loudly and bumping each other playfully. They instantly fell back into their old routine, walking around the preserve side by side.

A few years later, Jenny became sick again. When she ambled to a shady area and lay down in the thick underbrush, Shirley followed and stood by her. Two other sanctuary friends joined the vigil. At one point, the four celebrated Jenny's life with three hours of joy-filled vocalizing and trumpeting. The next day the vocalizing became soothing. Tara and Bunny stroked and comforted Jenny while Shirley withdrew in grief. She had a difficult time with Jenny's death.

Finally another circus outcast, an energetic new arrival named Misty, helped restore Shirley's spirits with her spinning and trumpeting. Shirley began to eat again, lifted her trunk up off the ground, and rejoined the herd.

We human beings have great compassion toward one another too. I see it exhibited often among friends and family. People sit together during surgeries, hospital stays, and death vigils. They pray, cry, stroke, remember, talk, and bring food. Even after loved ones have died, many caregivers return to support-group meetings—their sanctuary herd—to lend their empathy and encouragement to those still going through the caregiving experience.

Prayer: Loving Creator God, thank you for elephant trainers, elephants, and caregivers who show great compassion toward one another. Amen.

78

Fran

—◦◦◦—

Scripture Reading: Psalm 89:1-14

I will sing of your steadfast love, O LORD, forever;
with my mouth I will proclaim
your faithfulness to all generations.

Psalm 89:1

Ninety-one-year-old Fran phoned last night, and the conversation has been on my mind. Soon after her husband, Bill, died seven years ago, she went to live with her daughter and son-in-law. Fran has serious health problems and tells everyone Toni takes beautiful care of her. "I don't like being work and worry for her. I often dream about joining Bill soon in the glorious hereafter."

I felt a special bond with Fran when we participated in a women's Bible class. The bond became so strong she called me the morning she found Bill dead in his bed. I telephoned our pastor and arrived at Fran's house soon after he did. Fran thanked me again on the phone last night for being there during those difficult intimate family hours. I tried to convey to her the honor and blessing I received from the experience.

"The reason I am calling," Fran said, "is to tell you I understand the energy drain taking care of Bob is on you. Now, honey, you have to take care of yourself." Caring souls frequently give that advice, but somehow coming from the heart of Fran, the words gained significance. She was caregiver for Bill for thirty-two years! Bob has been sick ten years, and I have been a full-time caregiver for three years.

I listened to Fran describe how handsome Bill was and how deeply in love they were. He spent three and a half years serving in the armed forces during World War II. He called her when he was coming home, and she stood at the window of their small San Francisco apartment until she saw the cab pull up outside. Fran excitedly recalled how she ran out the door, and they hugged and kissed right there on the sidewalk. "But do you know what Bill did when we got inside? He took my hand and said, 'Honey, first, let us pray.' We got down on our knees in gratitude for his safe arrival back home. That's the kind of man he was. It was easy to take care of someone like that."

Bill and Fran modeled steadfast love and faithfulness in their marriage and in their relationship with God and the church. Their presence in my life has been a reflection of a loving, faithful I AM. They have proclaimed their faith to the generations. I am stirred to wonder who is watching me and what they see.

Before saying good-bye, I commented, "When I grow up, I want to be just like you, Fran." She erupted in laughter and said, "You're grown up, honey; you're almost seventy."

———

Prayer: Thank you, Abba Father, for friendships that proclaim your faithfulness to all generations. Amen.

79
Sheltering Wings

———✺———

Scripture Reading: Luke 13:31-35

*How often have I desired to gather your children together as a
hen gathers her brood under her wings, and
you were not willing!*

Luke 13:34b

During meditations today, the following scripture verse
grabbed my attention: "Let me abide in your tent forever, find
refuge under the shelter of your wings" (Ps. 61:4). If I'm going to
take shelter under wings, which wings would I choose? Certainly
not hummingbird or ostrich wings. Today I may be a tumbling
eaglet learning to fly and need strong wings to catch me, but I
don't want to soar with the eagles.

Every Christmas, I give each granddaughter an angel orna-
ment. Over the years a wide assortment of wings has graced
these angels—from fine porcelain to twigs. I could take refuge
under angel wings of long tapered white feathers, such as those
found in masterpieces of angels and chubby cherubs, but that's
not my style. Angel wings are out.

Perhaps creatures with wings strong enough to migrate across
continents and oceans would be a good choice. Ducks, geese, and
birds pass through this region seasonally, bringing great delight to
birders. Butterflies with wings of exquisite colors and intricate
patterns flock to my butterfly garden. None of these wings provide

the kind of shelter my bruised, responsibility-weary spirit longs to find.

When I was a small child, thunderstorms frightened me. My mother calmed me with this little rhyming verse: "Streaks of lightning, peals of thunder, old hen squats and chicks run under." As a youngster in Mississippi, I observed broods of little chicks and their mama hens. Chicks walk, scamper about, and know how to eat immediately upon hatching. Comfortable chicks make contented peeps, but chicks distressed from cold or hunger cheep loudly and insistently. When the mother hen makes her shrill clucks to warn of impending danger, those little balls of yellow fluff scurry like mad and duck under the mama's body. She squats right on top of them. I used to worry she would squish them, but the chicks always scrambled out round and perky as ever. They trusted their mother and stayed nearby until their feathers grew and they were mature enough to make it on their own.

Jesus longed to protect the people of Jerusalem but could not stop them from killing prophets and their Messiah. He desired to gather them like a hen gathers her brood under her wings. Sometimes life gets filled with sadness, dangers, and my own willful foolishness, but I know where to go to find shelter. I scurry under the outstretched wings of a trustworthy and compassionate God.

———————

Prayer: O Gracious Lord, you desire to protect and shelter us when we are overwhelmed by the hardships and trials of caring for a chronically ill person. May we never forget you are here for us. Amen.

80

Strawberries

—⊶⊷—

Scripture Reading: Proverbs 31:10-31

The heart of her husband trusts in her,
and he will have no lack of gain.
She does him good, and not harm,
all the days of her life.

Proverbs 31:11-12

For weeks we two caregivers had tried to schedule a time to visit. Today we finally managed an hour together. As we sat at the small round table in a neighborhood Starbucks, we sipped lattes and caught up on what was happening in each other's life. First of all I asked about the hand and wrist brace my friend was wearing. "Oh, it's from lifting John—just part of the way life is now."

Minutes later tears welled up in my eyes when the attractive, sixty-something, genteel lady informed me her husband had been placed in hospice last week. I knew he had Parkinson's disease and that life had been tough for her, but I was not prepared to learn the situation had become so grave.

Miriam is one of those women I label "a handmaiden of God." She is a professional church worker with a wide range of responsibilities—everything from teaching youth to visiting the sick to working at a night shelter and beyond. She could be the subject of the "Ode to a Capable Wife" found in today's scripture reading: "Strength and dignity are her clothing"; "she opens her hand to the poor"; "she opens her mouth with wisdom, and the teaching of kindness is on her tongue." I have great respect for this woman.

As she described the painful decision about hospice care, I listened with my heart. The nurse had come to her home for a scheduled evaluation and admission. When they told the husband, Miriam said it was like the air left his body and he went limp. John misunderstood that he would be reevaluated every thirty days. He thought they were telling him he only had that long to live. Miriam and the nurse tried to explain, but he remained despondent.

Suddenly John sat up straight. Miriam could tell he had slipped back into his own private world. He did not comprehend what was being said but simply looked up into his wife's beautiful blue eyes and asked, "May I please have some strawberries?"

Miriam told me he ate his strawberries, the nurse left, and the crisis ended. John never again balked about his hospice status.

Prayer: Lord God, may your handmaidens serve you with gladness and singleness of heart. May each one be blessed with the satisfaction of a job well done and the awareness of your delight in their loving devotion to others. Amen.

81
Washing Feet

━━━∞∞∞━━━

Scripture Reading: John 13:1-17

So if I, your Lord and Teacher, have washed your feet, you also ought to wash one another's feet.

John 13:14

Soon after Lana and Bud's fortieth wedding anniversary, Lana was diagnosed with dementia. Their devoted children and grandchildren assisted Bud tremendously over the next few years as Lana began a slow, steady decline. She approached the last days of her earthly pilgrimage, and the family opted to keep her at home under hospice care.

Nurses were present around the clock, except one morning. Two weeks before she died, the nurse's aide scheduled to bathe Lana had an emergency elsewhere. The bath was badly needed, so Bud decided he would go ahead. He set out clothes, diaper, and towels, got the bathroom heated, and proceeded to give his wife her bath.

Several male caregivers have remarked to me how difficult the business of personal hygiene has been for them. Many women have cared for children, the elderly, and the sick throughout their lives, but men generally have no experience in bathing and dressing others. Bud had a major challenge, especially with the bra. Thank goodness there were no panty hose. Bud struggled with the bath but somehow managed. While he was toweling off his wife, she studied him quizzically and spoke.

"Who are you?"

"I'm your husband, Bud."

"Have you ever bathed a woman before?"

"Yes, hundreds."

There was a long pause, and then his wife commented, "Didn't learn much, did ya?"

Lana had a delightful sense of humor before the dementia advanced. Bud and his son love to tell the bath story. Perhaps, they wistfully hope, she did know Bud and was only pulling one of her gentle teases.

I have a mental image of wife seated and husband kneeling in front of her drying her feet with a fluffy white towel. The image blurs until I see Bud as Jesus and Lana as one of the disciples. Washing guests' feet was a job for a household servant to carry out. But Jesus wrapped a towel around his waist, like the lowliest slave, and washed and dried his disciples' feet. He, God in the flesh, modeled the servant attitude we are called to imitate.

———————

Prayer: Gracious God, open our eyes to see our caring service to our loved ones as a holy calling to be you in the world. May we someday hear you whisper, "Well done, good and faithful servant." Amen.

82

Molly

—∞∞∞—

Scripture Reading: Psalm 104:14-24

O LORD, how manifold are your works!
In wisdom you have made them all;
the earth is full of your creatures.

Psalm 104:24

Three years ago Bob decided to rescue a medium-sized dog. The search ended on adoption day at a pet retail store when a woman walked in with a pretty, vivacious, female sheltie mix. Bob asked no questions, took the shot records, and told the distressed woman he would give the dog a good home. I purchased doggie dishes, food, and a goofy toy, while Bob began the first of countless conversations with "Molly."

The vet guessed the dog was a year old and gave her a clean bill of health. For several days, Bob was so busy getting Molly acclimated to her new surroundings he seemed to forget his pain. The dog adoption worked well until Molly chewed the elaborate needlework pillow I had made for an anniversary present. She chewed my red sandals, the sofa cushion, the back of Bob's recliner, and a quilt. Her doting master tried to console me, "She's a baby dog; she'll stop."

She stopped—two years later. By that time, she had taken up digging in the flower beds in the fenced backyard. Molly made amazing holes and large dirt piles adorned with my yellow irises and herb plants. Bob said, "She's trying to get to China; she'll stop." The digging hasn't stopped yet.

Bob and his dog are a study in contrasts. She is hyperactive; he is slow. Her barks are annoyingly loud; he speaks in soft deep tones. She is willful; he is a control freak. Molly jumps up on everyone and growls at the mail carrier. Her owner is laid-back. Bob feeds Molly from his plate. The one thing they have in common is a belief she's a person, not a dog. She's a marvelous companion, and the two sit for hours on the patio. I sometimes go to the window to secretly check on them. Molly sits close to his chair while he strokes, pats, talks, and sings to her.

I often wonder if Bob tells her about the emptiness he feels after retirement from a successful career. Maybe he explains the feelings of having his carefully crafted identity as a super salesman change to care receiver. Maybe he whispers to her about his pain, fear, and frustrations. Perhaps he talks about transience, learning to befriend impending death, and his belief in the good news. Then again, the talk may consist of daily platitudes. Maybe the songs are old Irish pub ditties. I'm not sure what Bob is conveying to her, but, for certain, Molly is engaged in holy listening.

Prayer: Thank you, Lord, for a cute little dog that delights a sick old man. Thank you for being our eternal supreme listener who hears the faintest whispers of our hearts and gives us peace. Amen.

83
Compassion

———8000———

Scripture Reading: Psalm 145:1-9

The LORD is gracious and merciful,
slow to anger and abounding in steadfast love.
The LORD is good to all,
and his compassion is over all that he has made.

Psalm 145:8-9

This psalmist talks a great deal about the mercy and justice of God. His enumeration of the Lord's attributes includes greatness, wondrous works, awesome deeds, abundant goodness, and righteousness. I especially appreciate the phrase "slow to anger and abounding in steadfast love" to describe God. During my meditation today, however, the word *compassion* jumped off the page.

Compassion combines *com*, which means "with," and *pati*, meaning "to suffer." It is the feeling for another's sorrow or hardship that leads to help, sympathy, pity (*The World Book Dictionary*). The compassion of Yahweh cultivates the notion that God is the Holy One who sees our fumbling, stumbling, suffering lives and suffers with us. The psalmist's God feels our feelings, understands how they affect us, commiserates, and stands in the struggles with us while we work through them.

I know many people who are forgiving. Compassionate people who simply stand by us when we hurt—not trying to talk us out of our painful challenges, not trying to convince us our attitudes are wrong, not demanding we pretend to be okay or someone we are not—are rare. They don't try to "fix" our lives or to give advice. They listen and help us sort things out for ourselves.

Joan Chittister writes: "Compassion pulls suffering out of the sufferer and love out of the listener." Healing and love are powerful by-products of a compassionate connection.

In the daily challenges and emotional roller coaster of caregiving, I wonder how many times I have asked my husband, "What did you say?" without ever looking up from what I was doing. I want desperately to grow that quality of soul that will respond to my care receiver's need for dignity, respect, and love. And not for his need alone but so that I can offer a compassionate ear to everyone who stands in front of me trying to have his or her heart truly heard.

A former professor at Loyola University, John Shea expresses awareness of the pervasive compassionate presence of God to human beings in these opening lines of a poem:

> If you had stayed
> tightfisted in the sky
> and watched us thrash
> with all the patience of a pipe smoker,
> I would pray
> like a golden bullet
> aimed at your heart.
> But the story says
> you cried
> and so heavy was the tear
> you fell with it to earth.

Our God is a compassionate God.

Prayer: Teach us, O Lord, to be more like you. Amen.

84
God's Big Toe

Scripture Reading: Genesis 11:1-9

Therefore it was called Babel, because there the LORD *con-fused the language of all the earth; and from there the* LORD *scattered them abroad over the face of all the earth.*

Genesis 11:9

At some point during every session of the Alzheimer's support group, someone will mention the need for humor as a way of maintaining caregiver sanity. Laughter is a lifeline. A healthy dose of humor does not lessen our respect or our commitment to our loved one. We are not laughing at them but at what has been said or done. If you find a pair of pajamas in the fridge, it's okay to laugh.

Perhaps this humorous story based on a little girl's concrete, literal, anthropomorphic image of God will add a chuckle to your day. It comes from a collection of short, funny allegories based on Bible stories by Rabbi Marc Gellman titled *Does God Have a Big Toe?* I summarize the title story:

> Life was good in a place called "Babel." That is until Arinna asked her mother this question: "Mommy, I have a big toe, and you have a big toe, and Daddy has a big toe. Does God have a big toe too?"
>
> The mother could have explained God is not human. God is unique, invisible, special, creator of the universe. God does not have a big toe since God is not a person. But

Mom was busy and told Arinna to go ask her father. When she asked her father, he was busy and told her to go ask Grandpa. Grandpa and his friend, Fred, were busy digging up weeds in a garden. Fred worked for the king, and he promised to ask him the next day.

The next day the king issued a proclamation to build a tower up to heaven so he could look at God's foot and see if he had a big toe. God was not pleased, so God mixed up the builders' language to stop construction. Chaos reigned by the end of the day as people were speaking different languages. Clusters of people who could speak the same language headed out of town together.

Arinna's family decided to leave town too with some people they could still understand. On the cart filled with their belongings, Arinna was quiet. Then she asked: "Mommy, I have a belly button, and you have a belly button, and Daddy has a belly button. Does God have a belly button too?"

Like the little girl, I am curious about God. How can God be so close and so far away at the same time? I know God is here with Bob and me, or else we would have broken down under the weight of our cares. Yet we can't begin to find language to express the limitlessness of such awesome Mysterious Love.

Prayer: God of Laughter and Joy, bless us with humor and uplifted spirits no matter what challenges may come with each new day. By the way, can you wiggle your nose? Amen.

85
It Ain't Over

⁊⁊⁊

Scripture Reading: Psalm 55:4-8, 22

Cast your burden on the LORD,
and he will sustain you;
he will never permit
the righteous to be moved.

Psalm 55:22

The pretty silver-haired lady spoke with emotion as she told the support group about her situation. "My husband's Alzheimer's progressed to the point I couldn't take care of him. I was living a nightmare. Now that he's in a care center, I go to visit and he begs to go home. He cries. When I leave him, I cry all the way home. Back at the house, I feel so alone and lost. It's terrible. You don't get over it. After they leave for a facility, you grieve. When are these waves of grief going to stop? And when will I stop feeling guilty? I play that 'what if' and 'I should have' game."

She lowered her head and concluded her comments with these words, "I thought when I got him in a facility and safe, it would be better. Remember they're still your responsibility, and 'it ain't over' as the saying goes."

A woman with white hair and porcelain complexion spoke next. She told about enrolling in a geriatric assessment program and getting the help she needed. "Everything was closing in on me. You know, I was the matriarch of the family, able to do it all. But my husband's Alzheimer's and putting him in a facility took a tremendous toll. I have a counselor now, and I'm getting better. I like talking to a professional—someone who doesn't know me."

The facilitator affirmed her: "Knowing you needed help and getting it show strength on your part. We applaud you and thank you for telling us about your wonderful resource."

Another group member spoke, "Sometimes I can manage, but other times I can't. I was sitting at the back of the church Sunday with tears in my eyes. The pastor walked by and saw me. She bent down and gently reminded me, 'Jesus cried. It's all right to cry.'"

Listening to the stories and remarks at support group sessions strikes a heart chord and heightens my respect for all caregivers. We are tested by "roaring lions" eager to devour our sanity, joy, confidence, and health. Each day I must rely more and more on a discipline of scripture study and prayer. My caregiving "career" has lasted for several years, but others have been caregivers for decades, with no end in sight. It ain't over, and it ain't easy. And it's all right to cry.

————————

Prayer: Compassionate Lord, it is comforting to know you care and you cry with us. Equip us with strength and patience to provide loving care to those who count on us. Amen.

86
God's Chair

———— ∞∞ ————

Scripture Reading: Psalm 47

For God is the king of all the earth;
sing praises with a psalm.

Psalm 47:7

My choice for today's reading comes from a group of psalms known as "the enthronement psalms." It is a hymn of praise celebrating God's rule over the nations. A procession of pilgrims, carrying the Ark of the Covenant, approaches the Temple on Mount Zion in Jerusalem with loud songs and shouts of joy. God sits on the holy throne, King of kingdoms, exalted above all the wonders the world has ever known.

These scriptures about God's reign from God's throne came to mind today because I made a connection between them and a little episode related during a support group session this morning. Gail told us her family had purchased a large, comfy, leather recliner for her husband, who has been diagnosed with Parkinson's disease and dementia. They were excited about being able to make his life more comfortable, but, after the chair was delivered, Peter would not sit in it.

"Peter, you are going to love this chair. Please, come try it out."

"No, I can't sit in that chair."

"Why not?"

"Because it is God's chair."

Gail and her son coaxed and begged, but the response was

always the same, "No, I cannot sit it that chair; that is God's chair."

Two days later, a daughter who lives far away phoned and learned about the chair. She asked to speak to her father.

"Dad, they tell me you have a beautiful new recliner, but you won't sit in it."

"I can't sit in that chair; that's God's chair."

"But, Dad, don't you know God would be very honored if you would sit in his special chair."

Peter went over, sat down in the recliner, leaned into the plush back cushion, and smiled. Many hours every day now, he sits contentedly in his new recliner, honoring God.

Prayer: King of all kings, ruler of all nations, may we, like Peter, honor our relationship with you and daily approach your throne with peaceful hearts and joyful praise. Amen.

87
Frogs in Cream

⸺⸺

Scripture Reading: Philippians 3:12-14

*This one thing I do: forgetting what lies behind and straining
forward to what lies ahead, I press on.*

Philippians 3:13b-14a

When I was a child, my brother and I often stayed with grand-parents on their farm in Mississippi. The one flaw in those idyllic days was my chore of churning butter. I hated the look and smell of clabbered milk. My tired arms felt like they were going to drop off onto the floor. My shoulders, head, and free spirit ached. The beads of perspiration formed across my nose and cheekbones, matching the pattern of my freckles. Each time I did the churn-ing, I feared the butter would fail to come. But it always did — eventually. In that bittersweet experience I learned the reward and discipline of perseverance.

I also learned a popular, anonymous poem during those years. My great-grandmother liked for me to stand on the little rug in front of her rocker by the fireplace and recite it. When I finished, she would give me a peppermint stick. The poem goes like this:

> Two frogs fell into a deep cream bowl;
> The one was wise, and a cheery soul.
> The other one took a gloomy view
> And bade his friend a sad adieu.

Said the other frog with a merry grin,
"I can't get out, but I won't give in;
I'll swim around 'til my strength is spent,
Then I will die the more content."

And as he swam, though ever it seemed,
His struggling began to churn the cream
Until on top of pure butter he stopped,
And out of the bowl he quickly hopped.

The moral, you ask? Oh, it's easily found!
If you can't get out, keep swimming around.

When I reflect on my life as a caregiver, I think about those two frogs and their opposing attitudes. People who are caring for a chronically ill or disabled person have fallen into a deep cream bowl. We have experienced times of crisis, frustration, disorientation, and disappointment. We have had losses: job, good health, homes, dreams, someone we love, and a sense of identity. Life, even when going well, is full of complexity and change.

No matter what is happening, like the little frogs, we have a choice in the way we respond to the experiences of life. Caregiving is a demanding teacher that invites you and me every day to learn about the depth of our faith and the breadth of God's love. It invites us to find the something more of ourselves, and our value as children of God. And so, we persevere and strain "forward to what lies ahead."

Prayer: Thank you, Lord, for teaching me the frog kick. May caregivers everywhere hold onto hope and keep swimming around until they find you. Amen.

88
Gospel Hour

—⊷∞⊶—

Scripture Reading: 1 Samuel 16:14-23

Whenever the evil spirit from God came upon Saul, David took the lyre and played it with his hand, and Saul would be relieved and feel better.

1 Samuel 16:23

A young man stood next to me at the doughnut table after worship service. He participated in our youth choir mission tour to nursing homes in the western United States. I said, "I bet you had a great time on tour. Tell me, what surprised you most?"

"Yeah, the trip was awesome. We'd go into these places and the staff would wheel all these old people in. Sometimes we went to their beds if they couldn't come to us. They looked like they were asleep and half dead. When we started singing, especially the old hymns, the residents would tap their fingers, mouth the words, and a few joined in. We were told some of them had not made a response of any kind in months. That was great, and it happened over and over everywhere we went."

I thanked John for his ministry on behalf of our church, and he smiled. "My pleasure, Ma'am."

Music offers a delightful resource for many memory-impaired or confused people. I know one man in a nursing home who sits almost comatose until placed in front of a piano. He can sing and play beautifully for hours, just as he did sixty years ago.

Stories about music pleasing and healing the mentally and physically challenged abound. Today's scripture story describes the shepherd boy David becoming acquainted with King Saul at the beginning of Saul's sufferings from mental illness, attributed in ancient times to *an evil spirit.* David played on his lyre (probably compositions found in the Psalms), and his music calmed and relieved King Saul.

Music offers inspiration to Bob and me also, and it provides something we can do together. For days ahead of Saturday, my husband will ask, "Is it *Gospel Hour* day?" He often tells me this hour is his favorite time of the entire week. I fix our TV trays, and we eat supper while enjoying the *Gaither Homecoming* television special. We clap, sing, and praise God along with the musicians. Bob delights in the show and encourages everyone to watch it.

Surgery to remove three neck vertebrae injured Bob's beautiful deep bass singing voice. He even had to retrain his muscles to swallow. Right after the surgery he could speak only in whispers, but slowly over the years Bob has regained his voice and his ability to sing those deep rich bass notes that tickle my heart.

> Then sings my soul, my Savior God to thee;
> how great thou art, how great thou art!

Prayer: Great and Good God, thank you for music with its amazing and unique ability to touch everyone—crying babies and wise octogenarians, robust athletes and frail invalids, choir members and those who are voiceless. Amen.

89

Helping Susie Cry

Scripture Reading: Jeremiah 8:18–9:1

For the hurt of my poor people I am hurt,
I mourn, and dismay has taken hold of me.

Jeremiah 8:21

In graduate school I took a course on Old Testament prophets. I chose to write one of my papers about Jeremiah, "The Weeping Prophet." He lived in a hideous period of Israel's history, the time of the Babylonian conquest. Jeremiah, a lonely and miserable man, was a reluctant prophet who struggled constantly with his vocation to prophesy. He delivered a bleak message: Jerusalem, Judah, Israel, and their citizens were sinful; their destruction was inevitable. His profound empathy caused him to weep and personally suffer over the imminent devastation of the land and the exile of its people.

Jeremiah despaired, "Is there no balm in Gilead?" Is there no resin from the balsam tree to heal the wounds of the brokenhearted in Transjordan? He cried not for his own troubles but for others who suffered, even those persons who brought about their own destruction by failing to repent and follow God. Later, however, when his words were about to come true, Jeremiah saw a more hopeful vision of the future when the Jews would return from exile and a new covenant with God would be established.

The "new day" did come with Christ Jesus, another prophet who wept for the city of Jerusalem and its inhabitants, for the family and friends of Lazarus, and for the heartsick and marginalized people of society. Jesus upheld a hopeful vision of a future kingdom where all persons share equally in the blessings and abundance. He offered himself as a balm "to make the wounded whole" and "to heal the sin-sick soul," as we sing in the familiar hymn "There Is a Balm in Gilead."

I heard a story about two little girls who enjoyed playing with their dolls together. One afternoon, Susie's doll got lost among the playthings and she began to cry hysterically. Mary also started to sob. The mother came in and wanted to know what was wrong. Mary explained Susie's doll got lost.

Mom asked, "If Susie's doll is missing, why are you crying, Mary?"

"Oh, I'm just helping Susie cry."

What a different kind of society we would have if people were more empathetic like Jeremiah, Jesus, and Susie. I want with all my heart to do something for my readers, so I promise to do the one thing I can, and that is to help you cry.

Prayer: God of Compassionate Tears, come heal the hurting. Give hope for an abundant life of joy and peace in the light of your mercy and grace. Amen.

90
Honor Your Father

—⟨∞⟩—

Scripture Reading: Deuteronomy 5:16; Ephesians 6:1-4

Honor your father and your mother,
as the LORD your God commanded you.

Deuteronomy 5:16a

Today I have been thinking about my father, deceased now for a number of years. At the end of his life, my mother took care of him with valuable assistance from my younger sister, who moved our parents into a little row house she owned only five minutes away from her home. Dad came to mind when I heard a comment from a friend this morning at church. He told me his ninety-four year-old father-in-law was driving a wedge between him and his wife. Because I make visits to see the old man, I know firsthand he is a complainer. I also know he is lonely and bored. I can only imagine his family's challenge.

Mr. Thomas has been moved to assisted living, but he calls all hours of the day and night to tell Paula and John he is dying. They rush over, spend hours in the ER, only to learn nothing is seriously wrong. The man has become a master at manipulating his daughter to get attention. No wonder the son-in-law is ready to explode with anger at both of them.

When children care for an elderly or impaired parent, the situation can become enormously complex. Issues of authority and power run askew of normalcy and cause friction. My heart aches for adult children in my support group who find themselves in these difficult role reversals. They feel sadness and grief at the losses they observe in someone they love and have looked up to. On a positive note, some families come closer together as adult children caregivers face these challenges. Parent and child spend quality time together and grow to know and love one another more deeply after a terminal diagnosis.

One middle-aged couple made the difficult decision to take the wife's father with early-stage Alzheimer's disease into their home. All went smoothly until one night when they were awakened by the lights and siren of a fire truck. Sniffing the air, they frantically ran to the window as the truck pulled up in front of their home. They were mystified since they had not called. The mystery was quickly solved when Dad appeared in the hall on his walker. He had initiated the phone call to 911 because he wanted someone to fix him a cup of coffee.

Prayer: Father God, relationships with earthly fathers can be complex and confusing. We pray for a strong measure of respect and humor even in the most exasperating of circumstances. May we come with grateful hearts to our shelter in you, Father, where we find steadfastness and unconditional love. Amen.

91
Male and Female

Scripture Reading: Genesis 1:26-31

So God created humankind in his image,
in the image of God he created them;
male and female he created them.

Genesis 1:27

This morning many attendees at the Alzheimer's/dementia support group meeting were men. They are unsung heroes in my eyes, and I wish the world could know them. The devotion to their spouses is a testimony to covenant marriage. Too bad many of the wives can't remember their past and are unable to appreciate the love and steadfastness of their mates.

Joel's wife was diagnosed with Alzheimer's when she was fifty-one years old. Her decline has been slow and steady. She is now sixty-four, and her husband has been shouldering all wifely responsibilities, plus her care, for many of the thirteen years since her diagnosis. He laughs about how long it took him to master getting Josie's panty hose on her. She refused to leave the house unless she was wearing them.

Joel continued to chuckle and said, "I'm still working on makeup. I do okay with the powder, but blush, eyebrows, and mascara are another thing. Josie likes to put the lipstick on herself. Sometimes it's almost to her ear. The longer I do all the wife stuff, the more I thank God I've only been a woman for a short while."

Then one of the women said, "But, Joel, you haven't tried having a baby yet."

Joel quickly replied, "No, not going to happen. We've already been through menopause."

The room reeled with rich laughter. The men laughed loudest of all. When the facilitator asked William how he was doing, he broke into a big smile and told the group about his seventieth birthday. His sons and their families were in town for Father's Day. They asked him if he had a rite of passage in mind for the landmark event. He told them he always imagined himself celebrating his big 7-0 skimming across the lake on water skis. His sons made that happen. William took his immobile wife and her equipment to a state park where the families gathered for a weekend together. Arrangements were made to stay in cabins with electricity. Family members prepared the food and took turns sitting with his wife.

William topped off his report with these words, "And I got up on the third attempt; I really skied."

Everyone cheered, but, again, the men cheered loudest of all. I've observed a kind of brotherhood among these males who share the pilgrimage experience of caring for their sick wives.

———————

Prayer: Everlasting and loving God, thank you for men who, in their daily rounds, reflect your faithfulness regardless of the capacity of the beloved to love back. Amen.

92
My Cup Overflows

———

Scripture Reading: Psalm 23

*You prepare a table before me
in the presence of my enemies;
you anoint my head with oil;
my cup overflows.*

Psalm 23:5

Our twelve-year-old grandson from Arkansas is visiting. He idolizes his twenty-year-old cousin and spends most of his time with that part of the family, but this is his day to hang out with us. He and Granpy helped me deliver Meals on Wheels this morning. After lunch, while my husband was resting, I took Drake on a tour of the ballpark in Arlington and to the Legends of the Game Museum. (One bonus of Bob's inability to entertain him the way he used to is that I now get my own one-on-one time with Drake.) A few hours spent with a grandchild makes all right with the world.

Later Drake showed me pictures from church camp and all sorts of fun Web sites on the Internet. While I fixed supper, he spent time with his grandfather looking at his massive coin collection. When we took Drake back to meet up with his cousin, I watched him hold his bent old Granpy's arm, hug him, and tell him, "I love you." There is a comfortable, easy, and natural bond between these two Noonan "men."

The Twenty-third Psalm conveys the psalmist's awareness of the goodness of God. The Lord prepares a table of provision for Israel in the wilderness and goes so far as to pour oil over the psalmist's head like an honored guest at the banquet. "My cup overflows" expresses the gratitude of a person who knows he is pursued by God's mercy and goodness rather than by enemies and persecutors.

A woman in my weekly Bible class gave me a copy of a poem, which, though simplistic, expresses the way I feel tonight.

My Cup Has Overflowed

I've never made a fortune and I might not make one now;
But it really doesn't matter, cause I'm happy anyhow.
I go along my journey, reaping better than I've sowed;
I'm drinking from the saucer, cause my cup has *overflowed*.

I don't have many riches and sometimes the going's tough;
But while my kids still love me, I think I'm rich enough.
I'll thank God for His blessings—the mercy He's
    bestowed;
I'm drinking from the saucer cause my cup has *overflowed*.

Grant me the strength and courage when the road
    grows very rough;
I'll not ask for other blessings, I'm already blessed enough.
May I never be too busy to help bear another's load;
I'm drinking from the saucer, cause my cup has *overflowed*.

Prayer: Good Shepherd, I sing a song of thanksgiving and praise for a few precious hours of making fond memories with our grandson. May he and your caregivers everywhere be blessed by many days when their cups overflow. Amen.

93

The Mustard Seed

oxxo

Scripture Reading: Luke 13:18-19

*[The kingdom of God] is like a mustard seed that someone
took and sowed in the garden.*

Luke 13:19

Rabbi Harold Kushner wrote *When Bad Things Happen to Good
People*, published in 1981, in memory of his son. Aaron was diagnosed at age three with a genetic disorder called progeria, which
causes rapid aging of the body. This tragic illness claims the life
of its sufferers at a young age—in Aaron's case, fourteen. Kushner struggled for an explanation of why life turns out a certain
way, or why things (good or bad) happen.

Rabbi Kushner has a remarkable ability to reconcile a common
Judeo-Christian view of God and causality with the randomness
of happenstance. He did not accept the premise that God sends
pain for someone's testing or improvement. Instead, he offered the
helpful point of view that God doesn't plan Alzheimer's, drive-by
shootings, child abuse, and killer hurricanes. The question is not
WHY things happen; they just do. The question is HOW to handle what comes our way. Kushner chose to cope with his grief and
loss, to struggle for hope, and to help others.

In the book, Rabbi Kushner tells a Chinese tale about a woman
whose only son died. Here is an abbreviated version of the story.
The woman asked a holy man, "What prayers or incantations can

bring my son back to life?" The man did not dismiss her but told her, "Fetch me a mustard seed from a home that has never known sorrow. We will use the seed to drive the sorrow out of your life."

The woman set out and came first to an impressive mansion. She knocked at the door, and inquired, "I am looking for a home that has never known sorrow. Is this the place?" They replied, "No, it can't be here" and proceeded to tell her all the trials they had endured. The woman asked herself, "Who is better able to help these people than I, who have experienced tragedy myself?" She comforted them for a while and then resumed her search. Whether she looked in poor places or wealthy homes, she repeatedly found stories of sadness and tragedy. As time went on, she became so involved in her ministry to others she forgot the quest for a magical mustard seed. She never realized it had, in fact, driven the sorrow out of her life.

The story reminds us that everyone is our brother and sister in suffering. No one comes from a home that has never known sorrow and heartache. We help one another because we know what it is like to be hurt by life.

Prayer: Lord God, your kingdom is like a mustard seed which, when planted, grows at a phenomenal rate. May we become sowers of little miracles. Amen.

94

Kathy's Dad

—⋙—

Scripture Reading: Jeremiah 31:10-13

I will comfort them, and give them gladness for sorrow.
Jeremiah 31:13b

A lovely, statuesque, middle-aged seminarian served her intern-ship at my church this year. As part of her training, Kathy preached two sermons within the context of congregational wor-ship. Sunday morning her words and Spirit-filled delivery touched me profoundly. I asked her permission to include a small portion of what she said about her visits with her father.

Kathy's father, diagnosed with Alzheimer's disease, made a gradual decline until he could no longer stay at home and had to be placed in an Alzheimer's unit of a nursing home. There he con-tinued the downward spiral into the stage where he no longer recognized members of his family. It broke Kathy's heart to visit him. He simply did not know who she was, and conversation was impossible.

Kathy went to the nursing home less frequently, but she con-tinued to go in spite of her feelings and her father's lack of recog-nition. Her dad developed the practice of crying when she came and also when she left. His tears puzzled her, and she thought her visits perhaps made matters worse for him. She decided to speak with his nurse about the situation.

"Dad cries when he sees me coming down the hall, and he cries when I leave. He cannot tell me what he thinks and feels anymore.

I can't decide if my visits upset him or what is going on. Should I stop coming?"

The nurse said, "Oh, no, dear, you must keep coming. He may not know who you are, but he knows what you are. When you enter, he knows Love has come to visit him, and he cries for joy. When you leave, he knows Love is walking out of his room, and he cries from sadness. Most of these patients do not remember and understand very much any more, but I have discovered they understand Love when they are around it. Obviously, you love your father, and when you come, he connects with that love."

Kathy left the nursing home that day with the calm assurance her dad was receiving wonderful care. The compassion and wisdom of his nurse comforted her. Her mourning was transformed into quiet confidence in the power of Love to conquer all, including the ravages of Alzheimer's disease.

Prayer: Great God of Compassion, I am grateful for your love that resides in Kathy's heart. Claim my heart too and teach me to walk in loving ministry to others, especially to my care receiver. Amen.

95

I've Got the Joy, Joy, Joy

⎯⎯⎯∞⎯⎯⎯

Scripture Reading: Psalm 65:5-13

The pastures of the wilderness overflow,
the hills gird themselves with joy,
the meadows clothe themselves with flocks,
the valleys deck themselves with grain,
they shout and sing together for joy.

Psalm 65:12-13

A cute blonde eight-year-old came up to the table where her father sat with us during coffee hour following Sunday services. She hugged her dad, who introduced her and bragged, "This is the joy of my life." I quickly understood why. She was perky and pretty, dressed in a brown and pink sparkly tee shirt that said, "50% Sweet. 50% Sassy. 100% Attitude." Her bubbly spirit was infectious, and she soon had everyone laughing with her humorous report about what had happened in Sunday school. She said, "We had fun today. We learned about Daniel and a fiery furnace and his buddies, Shadrach, Meshach, and Michelangelo."

"Joy" was the theme for the morning's worship service. The sermon, music, scripture, and offertory revolved around a celebration of the goodness of the Lord. A bouncy old song I haven't sung in years brought smiles and an attitude of playfulness.

> I've got the joy, joy, joy, joy down in my heart
> (Where?)

Down in my heart (Where?), down in my heart.
I've got the joy, joy, joy, joy down in my heart
    (Where?)
Down in my heart to stay.

With jazzy piano accompaniment, the singing was good old-fashioned fun for everyone. Smiles broke out on happy faces, especially when we sang the verse that begins, "If the devil doesn't like it, he can sit on a tack."

I thought about the merry song and cheery little girl several times this week. How often I feel totally joyless. Leaving my job to stay home with a chronically ill husband, watching his suffering and the changes forced on us—these experiences have taken a toll on my positive attitude.

As incredible as it sounds, after three years of this caregiving pilgrimage, I have come to believe joy can seek and find us in the midst of pain and sorrow, frustration and confusion. Joy calls and stretches out its arms. Joy comes from knowing God is as good as God's Word. God loves; God heals; God offers hope—hope that responds gustily in song with "I've got the joy, joy." The little girl's tee shirt is right; it's 100 percent attitude.

Prayer: Generous God, you know how often caregivers feel overwhelmed with their responsibilities. Inspire us with a spirit of joy and gladness worthy of your trust in us to care for our loved ones. Amen.

96

Gold Stars

Scripture Reading: Psalm 139:13-18

I praise you, for I am fearfully
and wonderfully made.
Wonderful are your works;
that I know very well.

Psalm 139:14

Decades ago Judy, my Al-Anon sponsor gave me an excellent workbook based on biblical teachings titled *The Twelve Steps: A Spiritual Journey*. With her guidance I progressed steadily until Step Four—"Made a searching and fearless moral inventory of ourselves." I spent hours writing down everything I could think of wrong with me. Judy scanned the handwritten pages of flaws, faults, and failures. She looked up at me and said, "This is okay, but you did only half the assignment."

"What do you mean, Judy? I can't imagine what I left out."

"Nell, don't you know you are God's wonderfully made child? Before our session next week, I want you to write down things good and right about yourself. That's part of your inventory too."

It was a tough week. I concluded from the experience that full human maturity may depend on two things: first, we always remember ourselves at our worst and, second, we never forget ourselves at our best. That kind of self-knowledge ranks simultaneously as one of life's greatest gifts and most humbling experiences. Both movements of self-reflection seem to originate with a sense of God's divine presence in our lives. We are made in the image of God and also fall short of our inherent goodness and beauty. According to the psalmist, God knows everything there is to know about us and loves us with an everlasting love anyway. How reassuring!

My husband and I share a primary care doctor. While performing a routine check-up this week, Dr. Jones asked me about Bob. I gave him my assessment. Then Dr. Jones said something surprising, "Nell, you are doing a great job taking care of him. You can take better care of yourself now because you have figured out what to do for Bob. I repeat, you are a great caregiver."

I wanted to cry my eyes out. I feel so angry and incompetent with this role more often than I care to admit. I appreciated the reminder from a doctor and a psalmist today that I am also wonderfully made and do a lot of things right. For the moment I feel like the child in this episode from *Splinters in My Pride* by Marilee Zdenek: "Once I knew a little girl who spent her own money to buy a box of gold stars and stuck every one of them on a piece of paper that had her name at the top."

Prayer: Loving and Great God, I wish I had crates of gold stars to give the millions of caregivers around the world. Keep us from being either too arrogant or too self-effacing. Lord God, may we someday hear you say, "Well done, good and faithful servant." Amen.

97
What a Little Thing

———

Scripture Reading: Psalm 145

*On the glorious splendor of your majesty,
and on your wondrous works,
I will meditate.*

Psalm 145:5

For months my thoughts, emotions, and spirit focused far too much on my losses. The biggest loss was leaving my job as a children's librarian to become a full-time caregiver, chauffeur, and nursemaid. Unhappy, angry and sad, I became a bore even to myself. It makes me shudder to think about the kind of companion I must have been to family, friends, and coworkers.

A combination of readings, thoughts, prayers, and a grandchild's comments worked on my mind and heart until an awareness broke through the muck and mire of ego entrenchment. I learned to hunt for, discover, and be surprised by all the wonderful little and big things that were good in my life. Every night before going to sleep, I wrote down three blessings in a daily log.

As the weeks went by, a more positive and happier person, I began a dance of gratitude with my Creator. Even the losses brought new awareness and appreciation. I could understand more deeply the psalmist who lived in a symphony of praise. Do not get me wrong. I am no Pollyanna and often feel sad, grumpy, and tired of my responsibilities. But at least most of the time I am on the path of acceptance and peace with my situation.

One of the gems I discovered in my readings was a poem by William Allingham (1824–1889), who was born in Donegal, Ireland. In 1870 he moved to London. He was an editor, poet, and man of letters who became popular for his folk song lyrics. I especially like this poem:

> Four ducks on a pond,
> A grass-bank beyond,
> A blue sky of spring,
> White clouds on the wing;
> What a little thing
> To remember for years —
> To remember with tears!

Today I have a special entry for my grateful journal. Bob and I sat in our usual place at the back of the church — my husband's motorized wheelchair parked next to me at the end of the pew. Bob reached over, took my hand, gently kissed it, and then placed it back in my lap. It was a little thing — a gift for me to remember with tears through eternity.

Prayer: Compassionate Creator God, I am overwhelmed by the gifts you are growing in me — a new depth of soul, a visionary eye, a symphonic ear, and a gladdened heart. Thank you for the softness emerging from the hard lessons of my life. Amen.

Exhaustion and Resurrection

—∞∞∞—

*Come to me, all you that are weary and are carrying
heavy burdens, and I will give you rest.*

Matthew 11:28

98

A Cup of Cold Water

—∞—

Scripture Reading: Matthew 25:34-40

If anyone gives even a cup of cold water to one of these little ones because he is my disciple, I tell you the truth, he will certainly not lose his reward.

Matthew 10:42, NIV

A persistent thirst is one manifestation of my husband's diabetes. He clutches a can of diet Coke constantly in case he needs to take a drink. I am puzzled about his compulsion to hold on to the can rather than to take a sip and set the can down, but that is what he does. He often falls asleep, and here we go again—wet shirt, jeans, chair, and carpet.

For the third time today I help him change his clothes. As I stifle the urge to scream, I reach for a towel and start to mop up. His spills are driving me crazy. "Oh, no, look at what you have done! *Again!* Why can't you just drink and put it down?"

I hate feeling so conflicted and awful. I glance across the room at the silver-haired man slumped in his leather recliner with a Coke puddle in his lap. My impulse is to yell and scold, but the last thing my husband needs is attack, criticism, or reminders of his clumsiness. He knows all too well about the changes in his ability to function normally. What would benefit him right now is help—a cup of cold water for his physical thirst and a gentle reminder of God's love for his spiritual dryness.

Jesus' example of giving a cup of cold water to a thirsty child provides a good model for caregivers. A child usually cannot—nor sees any reason to—return assistance to those who helped him or her. Our care receivers require us to give without expectation of repayment. However, there is compensation. I am reminded today God notices what I do (or don't do) as if God were the recipient of my acts of kindness.

Prayer: Dear Lord, release me and other caregivers from our frustration and our weariness. Teach us to see our care receivers as you do. When we focus on their limitations, we are not at peace. May we learn to take each day's happenings, even puddles of Coke, as opportunities to work for you. In that Spirit I know a blessing—a cup of cold water for both caregiver and care receiver—will refresh us hour by hour throughout every day. Amen.

99
A Familiar Voice

———

Scripture Reading: John 10:3-5, 11-17

He calls his own sheep by name . . . , and the sheep follow him because they know his voice.

John 10:3-4

No sooner had I resettled at the desk to finish paying bills than he started again. My husband called my name so many times from the other room I could not ignore him. His tone of voice let me know he was growing more anxious with each passing minute. I gritted my teeth, slammed the pen on the desktop, and tried to stuff my anger as I stomped down the hall.

"What's your problem? What do you want now?" I was sick of his interruptions, and I was stressed out by my additional responsibility for all the financial business he used to handle.

He said, "I'm sorry, but I can't find my glasses. Have you seen them?"

I snipped, "Why do you need your glasses? I thought you were going to take a nap."

"Well, I am, but I want to know where my glasses are first."

I mumbled to myself something about the absurdity of his request as I tramped around the house. I found the glasses on the kitchen table under the newspaper and hurried back to my agitated care receiver. He thanked me and calmed down when I put them in his hands.

Ten minutes later, he called again. I shouted, "What the heck do you want now? Stop calling me. I can't get anything done." My words combined with the stinging tone and higher volume of my voice made my aggravation and anger obvious.

At that moment I remembered the sage advice I heard from a soft-spoken older man whose wife has serious dementia. During a support group session he said, "If I can stay calm and am sensitive to the tone of my voice, she responds to that. She always responds to a friendly voice speaking her name. She likes a smile and a loving pat too. She can't help the way she is, but I can help the way I am."

I arose from the desk one more time and went to reassure my husband. "You seem to be fighting anxiety. Are you feeling afraid? I love you, and I am right here in the house with you. Everything's just fine."

I checked on him a few minutes later and found him peacefully asleep in his recliner, clutching his glasses.

Prayer: Good Shepherd, thank you for calling us by name. We know your voice and it calms us. We can trust you will take care of us. Use our voices to love and reassure others. May we respond eagerly when our name is called. Amen.

100

A Remarkable Lady

Scripture Reading: 2 Corinthians 1:3-5

. . . so that we may be able to console . . . with the consolation with which we ourselves are consoled by God.

2 Corinthians 1:4

I met an unforgettable person today—a petite, spry octogenarian with snow-white hair and crystal clear blue eyes. For years Polly cared for her husband, who suffered from Alzheimer's and problems associated with that difficult disease. She was instrumental in starting an incredible support group for caregivers and continues her group leadership even though her husband has been dead for some time now. I walked in the door of the room where the group meets, and she scurried over. Polly had never seen me before, but I quickly received a wonderful hug. Those amazing soul-filled eyes focused on me and spoke wordless words of hospitality and welcome.

I was offered a cup of coffee, a red napkin, and a large brownie on a red plate prepared in honor of a member's birthday. The group grew to about twenty or so caregivers. Polly skillfully facilitated the session. She began by sharing information about articles, educational materials, resource people, and upcoming workshops. I was astounded by her keen mind and the wealth of knowledge she dispensed quickly and succinctly.

Next, Polly went through the names on her roster and gave a report about her telephone conversations with them. She gave out her phone number so that new people would have it and issued an invitation to call her at any time. She said that her phone was quite busy but to keep trying. When asked by a woman in the group if she would like help with phoning her list before each meeting, Polly pulled her pretty soft teal-blue shawl around her shoulders and responded quickly. "Oh, no, thank you. I just love being connected with all of you and knowing how you are. That's why I like to call and why I hug you when you come in."

The session continued as Polly lovingly asked each person how he or she was doing. She called on members randomly rather than going around the room. I learned a phenomenal amount about caregiving that morning. I learned about courage, devotion, challenge—love.

Finding a support group, locating a sitter, and going to meetings are the best things you can do for yourself as a caregiver. You will garner wisdom, strength, and comfort from the people gathered to help one another. If you can attend a meeting only once a month or every two months, you still will feel enormous gratitude for the experience, as I do.

———————

Prayer: Gracious Other, thank you for Polly's faith and loving spirit. It is evident she consoles with that consolation of God by which she was consoled. She shows us that age is no barrier to effective ministry. As our days increase may we too grow in skills, wisdom, and compassion. Amen.

101
Abide in Me

—∞∞∞—

Scripture Reading: John 15:4-10

Abide in me as I abide in you. Just as the branch cannot bear fruit by itself unless it abides in the vine, neither can you unless you abide in me.

John 15:4

My husband's request for his glasses came three minutes after we returned from the doctor's office this morning. I hunted in vain. Then he remembered giving them to the nurse before he began his treatment. "Yes," I mumbled, but I surprised myself because it was not a loud, angry protest. I simply got in the car, drove back, and retrieved the glasses.

Bob said, "Thank you for getting my glasses," and it seemed the episode was over.

Because I normally overreact when these kinds of annoying interruptions happen, I pondered my calm reaction this morning until I figured out a reason for it. Before we left for the doctor's appointment, I had read an article about abiding in the presence of God. I desire a faithful discipleship in which I abide in Jesus and Jesus abides in me. However, my life as a caregiver brings interior sighs of resignation and moans of stubborn resentment more times than I care to acknowledge. Most people would not understand, but maybe some of you caregivers do. You will appreciate why it feels so good when the sighing pattern is broken. This morning I experienced a small victory.

Today's reality is what we have to accept and work with. What used to be is gone. When I accept today and retrieve a pair of eyeglasses without blame or rage, without resentment or displeasure, I feel a communion, an abiding, with Jesus. I am peaceful—for the moment.

———————

Prayer: Dear God: Father, Son, and Spirit, I continue to teeter precariously on the edge of allowing you to be in control of my life and letting my emotional hubris run amok to wreck my joy and peace. Teach us caregivers, Lord, to abide in you for the sake of both ourselves and our care receivers. Without you we become miserable and carry an ugly, unnecessary burden of regret and self-pity. With you, now that's something else—solace, blessing, and refreshment. Amen.

102
Bathroom Makeover

Scripture Reading: Exodus 2:1-10

She named him Moses, because, she said,
"I drew him out of the water."

Exodus 2:10b

Bob owned a house built in the 1970s and had lived there ten years when we married. The bones of the house were good, but I began systematic cosmetic remodeling. Dark paneling, dark brown carpeting, dark kitchen cabinets, and all things avocado, orange, and gold were replaced. Progress was slow because I was the sole laborer.

The last room to be updated was the hall bathroom. My affinity for the beach led me to select a seashore theme for the transformation. I owned some attractive framed artwork of seashells and beach scenes, a gorgeous embroidered "Footprints in the Sand" picture stitched by my sister-in-law, and an enormous shell collection. To complete the theme, I found a wallpaper border featuring seashells.

Stripping off the old metallic gold wallpaper in combination with a painting technique requiring four steps almost killed my enthusiasm for the project. Bob was still doing some woodwork at that time, and he made a tall, thin shelving unit out of weathered wood to hold rolled-up, crisp white towels and bath accessories. The new tile floor had a mottled design resembling sand. The results were quite appealing.

One morning soon after the makeover was finished, my husband had a grand mal seizure and stroke. Upon release from the hospital, he went into home health care. Early in his evaluation for the home health-care program, a nurse checked the house for safety and informed us how to adapt our home to Bob's physical needs. She told us the hall bathroom required another makeover.

Wall-mounted handlebars were installed everywhere. A free-standing raised toilet seat arrived to fit over the commode. A chair came for the bathtub, and a handheld spray nozzle replaced the showerhead. Rugs, some accessories, and the shelving unit had to be removed or relocated. So many unwelcome changes were taking over everything—even the beach bathroom.

When Pharaoh's daughter went to the river to bathe, she found a basket carrying a baby boy. She named him Moses because she drew him out of the water. Actually the name means "the one who draws out" and foretold his role as the leader to draw the Hebrews out of oppression and sorrow. Spirituals have used the biblical river illusion to describe the struggles we all face on earth. The river implies a long, hard journey followed by deliverance to a place of supreme respite, a promised land where all is peace. The spiritual "Deep River" reminds me my home is over Jordan at the gospel feast, not in a made-over bathroom.

Prayer: Draw us, Lord God, from our bath in the "deep river" of troubles and pettiness. Deliver us to the place where our souls crave to be. Grant us freedom in our homeward journey to the heart of our Deliverer. Amen.

103
Ceaseless Prayer

—∞—

Scripture Reading: 1 Thessalonians 5:16-24

Rejoice always, pray without ceasing. . . .
Do not quench the Spirit.

1 Thessalonians 5:16, 17, 19

Caregivers who can "rejoice always" are not human. That's too tough for anyone. Instructions to "pray without ceasing" are a tad easier to follow but still troublesome to practice. Pray—whether you feel like it or not? Pray—when you wonder if it does any good? Pray—when you're unsure God cares or bothers to listen? Pray—when you doubt God exists? Pray—even if it's not morning devotions, mealtime, or bedtime? According to today's scripture, the answer to my questions is unequivocally "Yes, pray, no matter what."

Ceaseless prayer is practical according to a wise children's song:

> Whisper a pray'r in the morning,
> Whisper a pray'r at noon,
> Whisper a pray'r in the evening
> To keep your heart in tune.
>
> God answers pray'r in the morning,
> God answers pray'r at noon
> God answers pray'r in the evening
> To keep your heart in tune.

When I don't feel like praying, I think of a story I heard about a remote village. It had all the necessary craftsmen, trades, and institutions. There were farmers, tailors, shoemakers, carpenters, and a doctor. There was a barber, a blacksmith, and a judge. One service was missing. There was no watchmaker.

Over time the clocks became inaccurate, and most owners decided to let them run down. Others chose to wind their clocks every day even though they were not accurate. One day a watchmaker arrived in town, and everyone rushed to him with their clocks. But the only ones he could repair were those that had been kept running. The abandoned timepieces had become too rusty to save.

Caregivers probably will not get rusty, since they tend to rely on prayer all hours of the day and night. It is an outburst of the heart, something done in our aloneness, a deep expression of ourselves. Our challenging lives are a natural catalyst to prayer. Yet none of us expects prayer to be a magic lamp—something to rub so that it will grant us special favors. What else can we do but pray? We are caught in circumstances beyond our control; we have to turn somewhere to survive. In prayer we expose ourselves to God. Prayer won't change our circumstances, but it may change us. It will keep our hearts in tune and our clocks set on God's time.

Prayer: Lord God who listens to our prayers ceaselessly, may we grow to be ceaseless pray-ers. We will be better caregivers if we do. Amen.

104
Graduation Day

———

Scripture Reading: Psalm 119:73-77

May your unfailing love be my comfort,
according to your promise to your servant,
Let your compassion come to me that I may live.

Psalm 119:76-77a, NIV

I held Bob's hand as we sat in the handicapped section of the huge college coliseum to watch our granddaughter Ellen receive her diploma. I could not help the flashback that rushed into my head and heart, one that prompted grateful praise for what was happening at that moment in our lives.

Twenty months earlier, after the ambulance drove away from the house, transporting my husband to the hospital, I reached for the phone and called our daughter. Granddaughter Ellen happened to be home between semesters, and the two soon joined me in the ER cubicle where Bob was being monitored. Our primary care doctor arrived on the scene and shared his concerns with us.

Wife, daughter, granddaughter took turns going to the bedside. We stroked Bob's hand and forehead and talked to him in hopes he would respond. We prayed; we prayed hard. I whispered in Bob's ear that he could not die—at least not until after Ellen's college graduation. He simply had to hang on for that landmark family event.

He did hang on. He learned to swallow again, to talk, to sit, to walk with a walker. Months and months of rehab and hard work, with the encouragement and expertise of numerous health care professionals, enabled him to recover enough to watch his oldest grandchild walk across the stage and receive her diploma. My eyes filled with tears of joy and gratitude.

Assurance in God's unfailing love had been the bedrock sustaining me during the long months of recovery after the seizures and strokes. No matter how dark and long the days and nights, I managed to hang on to the thin hope that God heard my cries. I know I could be sitting here without Bob in his wheelchair by my side. He even had another little episode in the motel early this morning. I made him promise he would not die and mess up Ellen's graduation day. He kept the promise.

My heart is filled to overflowing with gratitude for our granddaughter's accomplishments and the beautiful young woman of faith she has become. This is a doubly sweet and special day, because Bob was able to share it with me.

————————

Prayer: Almighty God and Father, we caregivers are learning how fragile our lives and the lives of our loved ones are. Help us put each day in your hands and release the future to your divine plan for our care receivers. Amen.

105
Not Allowed

—∞∞—

Scripture Reading: Matthew 25:34-40

I was sick and you took care of me.
Matthew 25:36b

Let me say it in plain terms: "I want to be sick today." Only someone who cares for a dependent child or an impaired person will appreciate fully what may sound strange to the rest of the populace.

I have a sore throat, pounding headache, stuffy nose, fever, and a miserable, achy body. If you sit in an ER or a doctor's waiting room often, it will come as no surprise to you that little germs and viruses are out there just waiting to pounce, and sooner or later they will get you. Probably I am more vulnerable because I am an exhausted, sleep-deprived caregiver with perpetual worries and responsibilities. The likely diagnosis is "caregiver burnout," but right now I don't care what the reason or cause might be. I just want to curl up in my bed and be sick.

Being ill is not an option for caregivers. We *must* get up and take care of our wards. Their welfare takes priority over everything else. The healthy spouse of a chronically ill person has no choice but to be well. I am coughing and hurting, but by golly I'm up on my feet fixing meals, dishing out meds, washing clothes, serving and ministering to my invalid husband. I wish I could act like a four-year-old child who stomps her foot and shouts, "My turn, no fair, it's *my* turn to be sick."

Later at night I lie in bed and wonder what would happen if I became seriously ill and could not take care of us. What if I died? Who would step up? Who would care? I won't entertain those futuristic possibilities tonight, although I know I should think through Plans A, B, and C. Some day soon, I promise, I will complete the legal kit I bought for recording everything the family needs to know about finances, wills, funerals, and the like. But at this moment the cough syrup seems to have taken effect. It's time to say prayers and go to sleep while Bob dozes in his recliner. Maybe tomorrow I won't care that sick days are not allowed with this job.

———————

Prayer: Lord God, Pain-bearer and Life-giver, I turn over my fears, struggles, and worries to you this night. I trust that Love incarnate, provided by our God who neither slumbers not sleeps, will enfold and hold us safely until the dawn. Amen.

Scripture Reading: Psalm 121

I lift up my eyes to the hills —
from where will my help come?
My help comes from the LORD,
who made heaven and earth.

Psalm 121:1-2

Caregiving can be overwhelming, a Sisyphean challenge. Sisyphus was a deceitful, cunning, conniving Greek mythological king. But this trickster eventually got his comeuppance. He was hauled down to Hades and condemned to an eternity of just deserts. His assignment was to roll a great boulder to the top of a hill. But after hard, frustrating toil and extreme physical exertion, every time Sisyphus reached the summit, the darn thing rolled back down.

The myth of Sisyphus has been interpreted in a wide variety of media ranging from an oil painting by sixteenth-century Italian Renaissance artist Titian to an essay by Camus in the 1940s. My thought upon hearing the myth was to question why this wily con man didn't con someone into pushing the boulder up the hill for him.

The thought also occurred to me that I might recruit help to assist with my caregiving challenge. I called a friend to meet for lunch. Our conversation caused me to pause and ask myself whether I had developed a case of Helper Syndrome. In my desire to be a good helper for my husband, Bob, I behave like a continual maternal fountain of common sense, advice, and instruction. My husband needs my help in many ways but not to do his thinking and feeling for him.

One way to show my love and support would be to listen patiently. I get bored with Bob's tedious discourses about health issues, aches, and pains. At times he exaggerates for dramatic effect. Nevertheless, he sometimes is providing me important information, and I have tuned out by the time he has spoken five words. I am not flogging myself on the back with a leather strap. My response to his diatribes is understandable and forgivable, but I need to respect his thoughts and feelings. To love is to listen, and to listen is to love.

Friends are helpers with their encouragement, food, visits, and gifts. But the greatest source of encouragement with my boulder comes from my Lord whose power turns each day's burden into a tiny pebble in my shoe. The Holy Spirit descends upon my life and makes me strong enough to keep going when I listen to the Silence of Love.

Prayer: God of Power and Might, when we care providers lift up our eyes to the hills, we can be sure you will be there. You help us carry heavy loads over mountains, and we are filled with gratitude. Amen.

107
I Am the Voice

∞∞

Scripture Reading: Ephesians 4:29-32

*Let no evil talk come out of your mouths, but only what is
useful for building up, as there is need, so that your words
may give grace to those who hear.*

Ephesians 4:29

I miss the good old days. Getting off to the doctor today was exhausting. We used to shower, dress, eat breakfast, and leave. Now a shower involves special equipment and an hour of time. Dressing means I set out clothes and help with buttons. Breakfast cannot begin until glucose values have been determined, a shot given, and meds taken. Then we put on Bob's hearing aids and find his eyeglasses. We retrieve a current list of meds and his wallet with ID and insurance cards. Bob dons a portable oxygen tank. A walker is used to get to the car. Later a motorized chair that lifts in and out of the car carries Bob to our final destination. Leaving home has evolved into a time-consuming, cumbersome process.

Bob no longer drives, so I have to take him everywhere he wants or needs to go. Outside home, I often become Bob's voice. He can speak more clearly now than he could a few months ago, but he still has some memory loss. I no longer can enjoy the luxury of reading a book in the waiting room. Bob wants me to be at his elbow in case he cannot find the words to express his thoughts or to fill in where his memory fails. The dependency is tough on both of us.

I often think about what characterizes a healthy caregiver/care receiver relationship. Bob, like most Americans, seems to bow at the altar of rugged individualism and independence. After all, these are key descriptors of our ethos. It is hard to admit vulnerability and weakness. When someone becomes chronically ill or impaired, the adjustment is difficult when he or she believes in the philosophy of "doing it for myself by myself."

A startling realization hit me. God depends on me—just as Bob does—to be helper, hands, voice, and lover in the vineyard. But I depend on God and am totally unable to go it alone. The more years I spend as a caregiver, the more I understand my radical dependence on Father, Son, and Spirit. I am weak, messy, and ugly on the inside—filled with anger, weariness, and resentment. I have to lean on the Everlasting Arms to keep me sane and somewhat civil in my caregiving role. The assurance God will not leave me to go it on my own allows me hang in there during the daily grind of survival.

———————

Prayer: Gracious God, care receivers may be dependent on us caregivers for many of their daily needs, but all of us are dependent on you. We are grateful for your constant presence and encouragement. Amen.

108
Arise, Shine

— ⌘ —

Scripture Reading: Isaiah 60:1-6, 9

Arise, shine; for your light has come,
and the glory of the Lord has risen upon you.

Isaiah 60:1

Deciding to leave my job to stay home with my husband was an excruciating process. Because money was tight, I feared we would not have what we needed. I especially worried about giving up the excellent health insurance and mail pharmacy program. But Bob's safety became an obsession for me when I was away in the workplace. I felt like a fly stuck in a web waiting to become someone's lunch—unable to resign yet worried sick about Bob's falls and debilitations.

I worked for a large municipality with excellent resources for employees and decided to avail myself of free counseling sessions offered to families under stress. After five weeks of counseling, I discerned it was time to resign and become a full-time caregiver. I plodded through a miserable adjustment.

Someone suggested *The Gift of Change: Spiritual Guidance for Living a Radically New Life* by Marianne Williamson. I generally dislike self-help books, but I stared down my reluctance to read this one. This book derives from the author's study of *A Course in Miracles*. Neither book meshes with my own theology, yet both provided useful insights for me.

Williamson writes: "A child grows whether or not he or she chooses to. At a certain point in life, however, we grow *only* if we choose to." She challenges her readers to face change not in resignation but in faith. "God so loves you, and loves the world, that He is sending it the person He has created you to be. . . . Bring the love of God, and you will bless. . . . Wherever you go, He will be there with you. And together, you will change the world."

I finished the book and the next day heard about a program for knitting preemie caps for two large charity hospitals. I purchased needles and yarn. Soon I prayed for the miracle baby who would receive my teeny cap. The next weekend at a garage sale I recruited a bored homebound neighbor to join me in knitting. Every morning I now ask what God has in mind for me this day. The variety of opportunities has been rich and unending.

Today's scripture appears in the church calendar for the Feast of Epiphany, which commemorates the arrival of the Magi with their gifts for the Christ Child (recorded in Matt. 2:1-12). I picture myself approaching the cooing infant in the hay-filled crib with my wee caps, my casseroles for a family in crisis, my letters to a cousin with cancer, and other daily offerings. I believe healthy spouses are invited to "Arise, shine; for your light has come." In addition to our care receivers, we can bring blessing and joy to someone somewhere today.

———————

Prayer: Shine in our hearts, Lord Jesus. Amen.

109

Acorn Anthem

—∞∞—

Scripture Reading: Isaiah 55:12-13

For you shall go out in joy,
  and be led back in peace;
the mountains and the hills before you
  shall burst into song,
  and all the trees of the field shall clap their hands.

Isaiah 55:12

In the March 1997 issue of *Country Living* was an article titled "The Man Who Planted Trees," by Jean Giono, based on his book by the same name. The tale begins in 1913 when the narrator, a twenty-year-old man, who remains anonymous, undertakes a hiking trip through Provence, France, and into the Alps to enjoy the wilderness.

The young man runs out of water in a barren valley. The only trace of civilization is an abandoned village with shells of houses and a tiny chapel with a crumbling steeple. He walks for hours, failing to find water. The narrator is saved when he encounters a middle-aged shepherd who takes him to a small stone cottage. There the shepherd draws water from a deep natural well he has constructed. The man speaks little as he shares his soup.

The young visitor asks to stay and rest, primarily because he is curious about this man. The shepherd, Elzeard Bouffier, had moved to the valley after the deaths of his son and wife. For years his habit has been the same: each evening he carefully selects one hundred acorns from thousands collected. On the following day, using an iron rod, he makes holes in which he plants the acorns.

Years later, after serving in World War I, the narrator, shell-shocked and depressed, returns to find the shepherd. He recovers in the peace and beauty of the vibrant valley and afterward continues to visit Elzeard annually, always amazed at the changes. Bouffier gradually restores the ruined ecosystem of the valley by singlehandedly cultivating a forest and making natural dams higher up in the mountains. The man who planted trees died peacefully in 1947 at the age of eighty-nine.

I love this inspiring fictional story. Real people have accomplished comparable results. Wangari Maathai, 2004 Nobel Peace Prize recipient, founded the Greenbelt Movement, which planted thirty million trees to restore the Kenyan ecosystem.

Caregiving requires us to learn ways of restoring our souls. A regimen of prayers, scripture readings, and devotions faithfully done each day can help us avoid burnout. I believe we bring joy to God's heart by faithful service in our simple daily tasks.

Prayer: Shepherd, Source of Restorations, show us how to create a vibrant environment for ourselves and our care receivers. May mountains sing anthems of praise and trees clap for joy because of restored ecosystems everywhere. Amen.

110
Like a Wheelbarrow

Scripture Reading: John 20:19-31

*"Blessed are those who have not seen and
yet have come to believe."*

John 20:29b

My remarkable ethnobotanist sister sent me a tee shirt purchased at the Fredericksburg Herb Farm in the Texas Hill Country. The front of the shirt displays a large green wheelbarrow. On
the back is the following sentence: "Faith is in many ways like a
wheelbarrow, you have to put some real push behind it to make
it work." This is one of those times to push.

My husband has a new brace for the upper half of his body
with a cuplike extension to support his chin. We have made many
trips to the orthotics supplier for the body mold, fittings, adjustments, and revisions. This is the fourth time we have been
through the brace program with different styles and different
businesses. The closet overflows with assorted neckpieces,
braces, and equipment. For over twenty-five years, since he
broke five vertebrae in his neck, Bob has pursued treatment and
correction. He believes *this* time he will be cured of his bent posture, protruding neck, and twisted spine.

In addition to being "braced," my husband does physical therapy at a downtown metropolitan hospital. Twice a week I drive
him, unload him and his chair, find parking in the busy garage,
and escort him to the rehab center. Most days he cannot complete

the exercises, but we show up. His therapist, patient, kind, and laid back, listens to the white-haired man with multiple diseases and challenges, as if my husband were the only person on earth.

The therapist has always been realistic in his prognosis, but Bob will not let go of his magical thinking. He believes he will stand tall and walk without walker or wheelchair, as he did decades ago. He holds on to that dream regardless of what doctors, skeptical wife, orthotists, and therapists say. God love this stubborn Irishman; he keeps on when all the evidence indicates his case is hopeless.

No matter how frustrated I get with Bob's pursuit of a cure, I admire the dogged determination that does not resign to his fate. I have faith in my husband, not his cure. I have faith in our love for each other, not in "happily ever after." I have faith in a Lord and God who accepts doubters. The longer I live this caregiver life, the more I believe that doubt is not the opposite of faith. It is simply one element of it. And so I give my doubts a silent nod and muster up enough courage to push the wheelbarrow to physical therapy sessions and appointments for brace adjustments.

Prayer: Today I cry out, like Thomas, "My Lord and my God!" I hold on to my belief that you are there, even though I cannot see you. Give us care providers courage to push the wheelbarrow even during times of unbelief or when our faith dims. Amen.

111
No Two Alike

———

Scripture Reading: Psalm 95:4-6

The sea is his, for he made it,
*   and the dry land, which his hands have formed.*
O come, let us worship and bow down,
*   let us kneel before the LORD, our Maker!*

Psalm 95:5-6

Trips to the beach have been a source of joy-filled therapy for my soul since I was a young child. Over the years I amassed a fine collection of shells. When we sold our house and moved into the duplex, boxes and jars of shells went into our garage sale. I gave the shells to two families of enthusiastic children, with their parents' permission. Their delight made parting with my seashells easier.

I allowed myself to retain only one bookcase shelf for seashells, but it is enough to satisfy my memories of collecting them and to tickle my wonder-filled admiration for these little gifts from the sea. They are even more cherished since Bob can no longer travel, and trips to the beach are a thing of the past.

I have given hundreds of sand dollars to Sunday-school students, workshop attendees, and members of Bible classes because of the shell's symbolism. The sand dollar has four "nail holes" and a larger hole signifying the place where Jesus was pierced by a Roman soldier's spear. One side of the shell has the imprint of what looks like an Easter lily with a star in its center to remind us of the star that appeared to the Magi. On the other side is etched a shape like a Christmas poinsettia. When the dollar is broken open, five little white doves of peace and goodwill are released. Isn't that like our awesome God to put The Love Story in a lowly shell?

Our Maker creates no two shells alike, just as our Lord makes no two persons alike. No two caregivers and no two care receivers are the same. Each is unique and responds to life experiences in a personal way. "No two alike" could be a mantra for support group sessions because it is spoken so often. Reactions to medicines, disease progression, and what works or doesn't work vary with each patient. Our care receivers are like my beautiful shells. Some are fragile and need to be handled gently. Some have a rugged shell. Some are chipped from being tossed about by bad storms.

We are reminded frequently that caregivers are not alike either. We each grieve differently. Each family member handles the loved one's debilitation in his or her own individual way and timeframe. We can access a wealth of helpful information available for us, but we must understand that our caregiving odyssey is individual and unique. We need to bring creativity and flexibility along with a generous dose of humor and patience to our ministry.

———————

Prayer: Come, Lord Jesus, and teach us how to tell your Love Story through loving care for our one-of-a-kind care receivers. Amen.

112
Age Angst

———

Scripture Reading: 2 Timothy 1:1-14

I am reminded of your sincere faith, a faith that lived first in your grandmother Lois and your mother Eunice and now, I am sure, lives in you.

2 Timothy 1:5

May is Older Americans Month, an observance first established in 1963 with a presidential proclamation by John F. Kennedy. I cannot for the life of me understand a reason for this designation. Perhaps it is a by-product of some kind of age angst. I guess we'll soon add Toddler Month and Preteen Month, but, truth be told, every person deserves respect and dignity every day all year long. Why not celebrate seniors all the time? Anyway, how many people are we talking about here?

According to the U.S. Census Bureau Newsroom and Data Center online fact sheet, there were 36.3 million people sixty-five and over in the United States on July 1, 2004. They accounted for 12 percent of the population. The number of people eighty-five and older was 4.9 million. The projected population of people sixty-five and over in the year 2050 is 86.7 million, or 21 percent of the total population.

This is a strange period in history. Americans get older every day as a nation, but we are increasingly anxious about the situation. We are intent on staying alive longer, but we are also dedicated to staying young, as if being young is preferable. We are a people in hot pursuit of the Youthful Grail and have forgotten about holiness and being faithful pilgrims.

It is generally believed we become better and wiser with age. We certainly aren't more nimble. These days I question whether it's better to be wise or to be nimble. I'm not always sure I have an easy answer. I use my age-defying moisture cream and dye my hair and think age is no proof I'm wiser or better or a joy to be around.

Someone commented that kids used to say, "Never trust anyone over thirty." Seniors say, "Anything less than fifty-two, and you're not playing with a full deck." I suppose both make a point, but I'm glad Paul and Timothy didn't adhere to those theories. When generations share their lives and wisdom with each other, the world is a richer place. Grandmother Lois, mother Eunice, and surrogate father Paul were there to nurture Timothy's faith. I want to be there for someone too.

As a caregiver, I want to model how to love well and grow old gracefully. It may be the greatest thing I ever get to teach the generation after me.

———————

Prayer: Rock of Ages, we pray that we may be a part of building faithful generations. May our aging and our caregiving reflect profound love for you and our care receivers. Amen.

113
Scary Blood Clot

Scripture Reading: Matthew 26:26-30

"This is my blood of the covenant, which is poured out for many for the forgiveness of sins."

Matthew 26:28

My husband called from his recliner, "Nell, come look at my leg. It hurts like the devil. I've had it elevated all afternoon, but it hasn't helped."

"What do you want to do, Bob? It's late Friday afternoon; the doctor's closed for the weekend. The ER wouldn't be good. How about if we go to the urgent care clinic? It's open until eight."

We discovered this clinic when Bob fell one Saturday morning. It's the only place, other than the ER, that takes Medicare. Plus it's near our new neighborhood. The clinic is run by two Vietnamese brothers. They came to the United States in the wave of refugee boat people in the late 1970s. These doctors rotate schedules, so one is always available.

The waiting room and exam rooms are spotless, and we've never had to wait more than an hour (unlike the ER, where the wait is never shorter than five hours, unless you enter on a gurney). The efficiency is a refreshing change from most emergency care.

Dr. Ngyuen examined Bob's leg. It resembled an overstuffed sausage about to explode and even had a bluish-gray color like an uncooked pork link. A finger touching the leg left an indentation that remained in the skin. Bob also yelped, jerked, and cried. We left with prescriptions and instructions for total bed rest until we returned Monday.

The doctor remained concerned at our next visit. We received a stronger prescription and instructions to return Wednesday. When the leg failed to improve, the doctor ordered a sonogram and X-rays. The culprit was found—a scary ole blood clot.

Bob began a series of shots and blood thinner treatments immediately. Our primary physician arranged for a home health nurse to collect blood samples, so we didn't have to make trips to the lab. He mentioned that sometimes support hose help sedentary care receivers who, like Bob, have insufficient blood circulation in their veins.

I located a long white surgical stocking left over from one of Bob's many surgeries and helped him put it on. The following morning, Bob shouted, "Nell, come see this. It's a miracle." And it was. For the first time in years, Bob's sausage leg was normal size with an ankle. Only then did he share his previous fears about losing his leg, but the blood was flowing again now and healing his body. I never revealed I had entertained those same frightening thoughts.

The change was miraculous. But the greater miracle is the daily redemption we find for our souls in the blood that flows from Calvary. No matter how much our bodies decline and fail, Jesus unfailingly provides us with the hope and promise of salvation.

_____

Prayer: Lord of Love and Healing, each time we drink from the Communion cup, may we be mindful and grateful for the blood of the New Covenant that makes us whole. Amen.

114
Sundowners
———

Scripture Reading: 2 Corinthians 4:1-6

For it is the God who said, "Let light shine out of darkness,"
who has shone in our hearts to give the light of the knowledge
of the glory of God in the face of Jesus Christ.

2 Corinthians 4:6

The subject of "sundowners" came up during a recent Alzheimer's/dementia support group session. I have not faced this aspect of caregiving with my husband, but many there deal with Sundowner's Syndrome, a difficult and dangerous dilemma.

People with some forms of dementia can develop behavior problems that occur in the late afternoon or evening, times when caregivers are the most tired. In cases of serious dementia, the symptoms may continue throughout the night. Research continues, but at this point Sundowner's Syndrome remains a mystery to medical science.

Support group members have described manifestations of the syndrome: rapid mood changes, anger, crying, agitation, pacing, rocking, fear, and stubbornness. In more severe cases, hallucinations, hiding things, paranoia, violence, and wandering occur. For some in the group, these symptoms forced the heart-wrenching decision to have their care receiver institutionalized.

Caregivers can become ingenious and resourceful in coping with these various symptoms. Several turn lamps on before sunlight fades, and many keep night-lights on at all times. One woman observed that her husband calms down when she plays soft, relaxing music, especially CDs of ocean waves and birdsongs. Everyone talks about the importance of maintaining routine and keeping life simple. Fatigue seems to be a catalyst for episodes, so exercise needs to be light to moderate. One group member learned not to pair a trip to the doctor with grocery shopping.

The busyness surrounding after-school activities with children and supper preparation is hard on families with youth and a demented parent under the same roof. One family arranges for someone to take the grandfather for a walk at a neighborhood park or, in the case of inclement weather, to go to the public library where he can listen to music on his personal headset. The man is brought back home when everyone is sitting down to dinner.

William told us his wife is having a new symptom between six and seven every evening. Her body suddenly becomes stiff like a board, and she slides out of her wheelchair. Someone asked if he knew about the Barton chair that can convert to a prone position. She took a video from her purse and handed it to him.

Support group sessions fascinate me. The Holy Spirit blows about the room and brings God's people to shed divine light into the dark corners of their Herculean difficulties, even after the sun goes down.

Prayer: All-seeing God, this little light of mine may not be a very big light, but even a tiny night-light can penetrate someone's darkness. Use us, gracious God, to your glory. Amen.

115
Tevye's Prayer

Scripture Reading: Psalm 28

To you, O LORD, I call;
my rock, do not refuse to hear me,
for if you are silent to me,
I shall be like those who go down to the Pit.

Psalm 28:1

My favorite musical movie is *Fiddler on the Roof*, set in czarist Russia in 1905. The original show opened on Broadway in 1964, and the film came out in 1971. The story revolves around Tevye, a philosophical village milkman and father of five daughters. He tries to maintain his family and religious traditions while the world around him changes rapidly. He must cope with the strong-willed actions of his three older daughters, whose choice of husbands moves them further and further away from established customs. Additionally, the czar has issued an edict that upends his village.

In Act I, because Tevye's poor horse is lame, he must pull the milk cart himself. He stops and asks God, "Who would it hurt if I were a rich man?" Rotund Zero Mostel portrayed Tevye with such honest earthiness and passion that my husband, in his robust, agile years, liked to imitate him.

> Lord, . . . would it spoil some vast eternal plan if I
> were a wealthy man? . . .

If I were a biddy-biddy rich, daidle deedle daidle
daidle man.

Prayer is natural to Tevye—no need for explanation or justification. He speaks spontaneously and forthrightly to a God who is as real to him as his own wife, and with whom he is more comfortable than he is with his own daughters. He makes his honest petition with humor tinged with a dash of pathos. I understand this kind of intimate, frank prayer to God when addressing personal needs. I often engage in petitions related to mundane matters.

As the drama progresses, we realize the play is an allegory of the purification and maturation of Tevye. His world collapses. His final flight from his ancestral home is symbolic of the erosion of the traditional values that gave his life meaning and made his faith secure. To continue to encounter God requires internal change that comes out of a rigorous "shaking of the foundations."

The play's title is derived from a Marc Chagall painting. The fiddler is a metaphor for survival in a life of uncertainty and imbalance via tradition and joyfulness.

My world as I knew it, and as I expected it to be, has been turned inside out. Caregiving stretches me; I long for the "good old days." But God asks me to grow beyond a simplistic "whistling in the dark" faith. Like Tevye, I'm not certain where I'm going, but in this life we are always "on the way" to new depths with God.

———————

Prayer: Lord, no matter how chaotic our world becomes, we can always count on your changelessness and steadfast love. Thank you. Amen.

116

Bona Dea

Scripture Reading: Ezekiel 17:22-24

*In the shade of its branches will nest
winged creatures of every kind.*

Ezekiel 17:23

A tremendous effort was required to attend our granddaughter's wedding. Bob decided he couldn't handle the six-hour drive and activities surrounding the happy event. I am blessed to have a great senior care service as a resource. Arrangements were made for help with his meals and meds as well as providing several hours of companionship, so I could go. Bob does not like "being treated like a child who needs a sitter," but he had no choice. I was determined to attend the wedding. We compromised: I agreed to let him stay alone at night from 9:00 p.m. until 7:00 a.m. the next morning.

I cruised along in the car enjoying the scenery with almost no stops—temperature and radio settings where I like them. The four-month-old grandson and I hung out during the rehearsal, and then we joined the wedding party for the rehearsal dinner. Back at the motel after a telephone call to Bob, I slept soundly.

The next morning I browsed through brochures from the Arkansas welcome center to see if there were hiking trails nearby. I chose Lake Dardanelle, only six miles away. A sign pointing to Bona Dea Trails and Wildlife Sanctuary caught my eye, and I parked the car. The hard-surface trail, designed for jogging and fitness, is also excellent for easy walking. I saw marshy areas, meadows, bullfrog ponds, sloughs, forests, and rocky cliffs with caves.

In addition to the wide diversity in topography, the flora provided magnificent variety. Wildflowers, trees, shrubs, and grasses were a feast for the eyes. Birds and wildlife were prevalent. Cedar trees attracted hundreds of cardinals that flashed red among dark green feathery branches. I loved breathing fresh, moisture-filled air after a rain shower.

I walked and walked, totally entranced by God's creative wonders. Finally it hit me: this is wedding day! I needed to go but couldn't find my way out. I passed the Rabbit Run sign a third time. A jogger and her little dog came by and gave me directions. I walked faster. Another jogger came and told me to go right at every fork in the trail. He told me it was the shortest way, but I had another mile to go. I walked as fast as I could and managed to arrive at the chapel with time to spare. Later at the reception our son, a marathoner who runs at Bona Dea, explained that interconnecting loops create trails anywhere from a half mile up to five and a half miles in length.

My life back home has loops—Bob, dog Molly, church, family, writers' group, teaching Bible, gardening, reading, and praying. Often I am confused and wander. However, the scenery there is also intriguing and points to an awesome Creator.

Prayer: My heart sings with gratitude for my three hours "lost" in Bona Dea. Thank you for the assurance that all living things, including caregivers, can always find sanctuary in their Maker. Amen.

117
Chicken Potpie

───⮟───

Scripture Reading: Romans 15:1-6

Each of us must please our neighbor for the good purpose of building up the neighbor.

Romans 15:2

A delightful, vivacious friend approached me with a warm smile and cheery greeting after the Sunday church service. I was getting doughnuts and coffee for my husband, who was seated at a large round table with old friends and would not hear our conversation. Janet nodded his way and commented that he seemed to be making good progress.

"But, you look tired. How are *you* doing, really?"

It is always about Bob—his health, his pain, his doctors, his depression, his rehab. No one asks about me, and I was so startled when it happened I didn't know how to respond. Truth be told, I often suffer from depression, loneliness, and fatigue. I was not honest with my reply when I told her I was doing fine.

Janet said, "I'm bringing you supper tomorrow."

"Oh, you don't need to do that. I'm okay, and everyone has been so generous with meals, phone calls, prayers, and cards when Bob was so seriously sick. I appreciate the help more than anyone will know, but we are past the critical stage and rocking along okay now. No doubt, there will be a day when we will need help again. Thanks for your thoughtful offer, but we're fine."

Softly, but firmly, Janet stated, "I'm bringing you supper tomorrow."

I find it difficult to accept help and kindnesses from others. I like to take a homemade cake, sliced roast, or tasty casserole to someone going through difficult times, but allowing someone to show that kind of loving generosity to me is hard. I am a giver, who is uncomfortable as a receiver.

The next morning my husband went out to get the newspaper, lost his balance, and fell. Head wounds bleed like crazy, so I wrapped a beach towel around his head, and took him to the ER. Five hours and nine staples later, we returned home. He slept while I "mumbled" about the circumstances of my life.

Late in the afternoon the doorbell rang. Janet stood at the door with a huge picnic basket laden with a gourmet meal. As I looked at the feast she placed on our kitchen counter, I felt overwhelmed and ashamed that I had tried to shut her out of my pain. I needed my precious friend and her exquisite comfort food. Janet listened as I poured out my feelings, and later that evening Bob and I enjoyed the most delicious chicken potpie ever.

Prayer: Great and compassionate God, I confess to you my sin of prideful self-reliance. May we caregivers never distance your friends and their priceless, loving gifts. Teach us to receive graciously. Amen.

118
Courage

—⋙—

Scripture Reading: Psalm 31:19-24

*Be strong, and let your heart take courage,
all you who wait for the LORD.*

Psalm 31:24

Today I felt I had landed in the fourth chapter of Lewis Carroll's *Alice Through the Looking-Glass*. I became Alice trying to find her way back home when she met Tweedledum and Tweedledee. She asked them for directions, only to have Tweedledee respond by reciting "The Walrus and the Carpenter." The craziness continued when Tweedledum accused Tweedledee of spoiling his new rattle, and they agreed to have a battle. "Battle" requires special gear, so they collected bolsters, blankets, rugs, and assorted items to wear.

Alice helped the two dress and was amused when Tweedledee asked her to arrange a bolster to protect his neck because "it's one of the most serious things that can possibly happen to one in a battle—to get one's head cut off." What follows next is one of my favorite passages in the entire book. Tweedledum asks Alice, "Do I look very pale?"

> "Well—yes—a little," Alice replied gently.
> "I'm very brave, generally," he went on in a low
>   voice: "only to-day I happen to have a
>   headache."

"And I've got a toothache!" said Tweedledee, who
    had overheard the remark. "I'm far worse than
    you!"
"Then you'd better not fight to-day," said Alice.

I thought about Lewis Carroll's story and my topsy-turvy
world after walking the dog this morning. Bob announced he was
having breathing problems and wanted to go to the doctor. A few
questions later, I realized it was not an emergency. Miraculously,
our primary doctor could see him in two hours. Then I became
angry about the situation. I spend most of my life taking care of
Bob, and it's such a frustrating job. I know what's going to happen. The doc will order more tests, which will be inconclusive
and unhelpful. Time and money wasted—*again*.

Being a well spouse of a debilitated person takes a whale of a
lot of courage. This is not some kind of romantic courage, such as
in brave men and women risking their lives in combat or dangerous circumstances. Sometimes courage is learning to endure
those things we cannot change. It is the willingness to keep striving on when there is not one shred of evidence to suggest we will
be successful.

Prayer: Abba Father, this has been a difficult, frustrating day.
Generally I am brave, but today I want to be Tweedledum
and excuse myself from the "battle" with a headache. The
strength we caregivers need comes from you. Grant us
courage to reach out, take your hand, and keep going. Amen.

119
Crossword Puzzles

───❦───

Scripture Reading: John 1:1-5

*In the beginning was the Word, and the Word was with God,
and the Word was God.*

John 1:1

Bob loves crossword puzzles. It was a terrible loss to him when he couldn't do them for many months because of double vision. The words, numbers, and spaces were one big blur, and the more he studied them, the worse the condition became.

More than a year has passed since his cataracts were removed and he received implants. The principal gift of that successful surgery has been the ability to read the newspaper and do crossword puzzles again. Bob's books of the *New York Times* puzzles, pens, and those correction gadgets that cover up mistakes have resurfaced in his favorite "hanging out" places around the house.

I will never cease to be amazed that Bob's illness has affected his short-term memory, yet he can pull up obscure words to fill in those tiny squares. He cannot recall the name of his primary disease, *diabetes*, nor remember the green vegetable on his plate is called *broccoli*. But he can remember the name of one of the five Norse royals or the weeping mother of myth to complete the puzzle Downs. Who knows that stuff? Who cares? The answer: puzzle lovers and those who design them with their secret conspiracy to intimidate us "normal" folk.

Attempting to fill in a crossword is an appropriate metaphor for my daily life as a caregiver. I try to make sense out of what seems incongruous, absurd, and horrifying while I hang on to a wispy hope God will fill in my crossword puzzles with words like *order, peace, love, patience,* and *joy.* I love the Lord Jesus, but sometimes the Word seems transcendent and floating about the spacious cosmos far from the tear-drenched pillow where I lay down my weary head.

At other times, Immanuel, the Word made flesh, is so present, I can easily fill in the empty spaces of my daily grind with God's company, tenderness, and compassion. One reason I love the Lord so much is being able to sense this amazing God here, near, personal, calling my name. And not here for me alone. It's an awesome God, this Judeo-Christian God, who knows us intimately and loves us individually as if each one of us is a one and only dearest child.

My daily puzzles change when I fill in the blanks with "beautiful words, wonderful words, wonderful words of life" (to quote a familiar hymn). Words like *cross, grace, forgiveness, love,* and *hope* come to mind.

———————

Prayer: O Word of God incarnate, you bless with words assuring: "I am with you to the end." We praise you, Lord, and ask that our words be a blessing in your service. Amen.

120

Masks Removed

—◦◦◦—

Scripture Reading: 3 John 2-4

I have no greater joy than this, to hear that my children are walking in the truth.

3 John 4

When I was a little girl and behaving like a brat, my grandmother told me real ladies do not let their ugly side show. Pretending became second nature with me. I gave the impression I was secure—all sunny and unruffled, inside and out. Confidence was my name and coolness my game. I wore a thousand masks and projected a cool facade. Beneath the surface, behind the disguises, dwelled the real me in confusion, fear, and aloneness.

Through the years I played my desperate pretending game of assurance without, but felt like a trembling child within. I idly chattered in suave tones of surface talk. I told people everything that's really nothing, and nothing of everything. Many months I simply did not know how to deal with Bob's health issues, leaving my job, and becoming a full-time caregiver. I camouflaged the truth with thin, pleasant smiles and superficial jabber.

Over time a metamorphosis occurred. I passed through a stage of denial and anger about the changes in our lives, then a time of profound grief over all the losses, and finally a tough, tentative acceptance of what was. This ongoing transformation began one morning in my prayer chair. I imagined God the Father wiping away the blank stare of deadness from my eyes and whispering a call back to aliveness. He was kind, gentle, and encouraging. Abba Father assured me he was present and really cared. My heart began to grow wings, very small wings, feeble ones but wings nonetheless. The more real I became, the happier I grew.

These days *superficial* and *phony* are two adjectives I don't want associated with my name. I work constantly to make every interaction, whether in person or through my written words, genuine, spontaneous and authentic. I want to share the truth of my pilgrimage. That does not mean I run out to make a sideline career of telling and retelling the details of my story to dramatize and wallow in personal history. I want to discern when telling my story serves a good purpose. Otherwise, I pray for silence and a compassionate ear for others who need an invitation to remove their own masks.

I am grateful for the lessons I am learning from my experiences as a caregiver. The masquerade is over. It's fun to watch paper dolls become real flesh and blood.

Prayer: Thank you, Almighty God, for embracing and nurturing the real me. May we caregivers be authentic in every word and action as we seek to share your love story with those who need to hear it. Amen.

121
Muck, Muck, Go Away

———✺———

Scripture Reading: John 21:1-14

*When they [the fishermen disciples] had gone ashore, they
saw a charcoal fire there, with fish on it, and bread. . . .
Jesus said to them, "Come and have breakfast."*

John 21:9, 12

According to an article by Ted O'Callahan in the September–
October 2007 issue of *Audubon*, muckrakers have invaded
Florida. A drought caused record low water levels in Lake Okee-
chobee, "the heart and lungs of the Everglades," and exposed a
layer of phosphorous-laden muck along the bottom of the 730-
square-mile lake. The South Florida Water Management District
actually found something good in this situation: they could access
the muck. Through a state initiative and a speedy action plan,
swarms of bulldozers and backhoes scraped off 1.9 million cubic
yards of muck and hauled it away. That's enough waste to fill the
Miami Dolphins' stadium.

The original plan called for distributing the nutrient-rich muck
to landowners, but elevated levels of arsenic made it unclear what
would happen to the mounds of toxic sediment stored near the
lake. One hundred fifty thousand tons, largely the result of fertilizer runoff and land development that reshaped the hydrology,
were removed from the lake. Approximately 50,000 tons remain
and need extraction.

Since the de-mucking, butterweed, bulrush, and cockspur grass have taken hold in the lake. When the drought ends and the lake refills, biologists expect increases in the numbers of birds such as white ibises, tricolored herons, and snowy egrets. The restored areas will support fish such as bass and crappie and improve food sources for several endangered species of wildlife.

Muck maladies require more than large Band-Aids. The Everglades continues to slowly die. Efforts at restoration are costly and probably too little too late. The decline of healthy ecosystems worldwide is scary and scandalous. It is frustrating to want to do something and not know what to do. That frustration begs the question of my participation in the destruction of healthy relationships with nature, other people, and the Creator. What muck do I arrogantly and ignorantly contribute?

When I think about my caregiving ecosystem, I wonder how I might keep the muck away. I get impatient, cranky, frustrated, resentful, tired, and downright bored with my situation. Emotions of anger and fear muck up my insides and block my channels for Christlike care to my dear husband. That's when I fall on my knees and plead with the Lord to remove the deadly gunk that interferes with self-offering love.

Prayer: Transform us, dear God, and help us cultivate a healthier environment for our care receivers and ourselves. Teach us how we may participate in building a world where Jesus will stand on the shores of restored, regenerated lakes calling his disciples to a char-cooked breakfast. Amen.

122
Master Builder

Scripture Reading: 1 Corinthians 3:10-17

*Do you not know that you are God's temple
and that God's Spirit dwells in you?*

1 Corinthians 3:16

One of my unfulfilled dreams is to tour English churches and gardens. First stop on my ideal itinerary would be Saint Paul's Cathedral.

The Great Fire of 1666 gutted the medieval City of London inside the old Roman city wall. Fire consumed over 13,000 homes that housed approximately 70,000 of the 80,000 in population. It also destroyed eighty-seven parish churches, Saint Paul's Cathedral, and numerous other buildings. Two-thirds of the city was reduced to a wasteland. The death toll is unknown because many bodies were cremated in the intense heat.

Christopher Wren (1632–1723), designer, astronomer, Oxford professor, geometrician, and architect, immediately worked out a plan for rebuilding Saint Paul's. He submitted it to Charles II, and construction started in 1673. His son, Christopher Wren Jr., completed the building in 1711, thirty-nine years later. Wren Sr. also designed fifty-three parish churches and many secular buildings. When he died at age ninety, his remains were placed in the cathedral crypt. His namesake and heir wrote the famous epitaph: *Lector, Si Monumentum Requiris Circumspice* ("Reader, if you seek his monument, look around").

A popular story reported that Sir Christopher Wren had enjoyed making tours of the construction site to observe the work in progress. On one occasion, he approached a man at work and asked him, "What are you doing?" The man replied, "I am cutting this stone to a size and shape to fit in a certain place." Wren strolled on and came to a second man and asked him the same question. This worker replied, "I am earning enough money to support my family." Wren proceeded to a third man and again posed the question, "What are you doing?" The man stopped, straightened up, and answered, "I am helping Sir Christopher Wren build Saint Paul's Cathedral."

Our point of view profoundly affects our attitude about the work we do. Today's scripture affirms this statement. Paul writes, "According to the grace of God given to me, like a skilled master builder I laid a foundation. . . . For no one can lay any foundation other than the one that has been laid; that foundation is Jesus Christ." With the help of the Holy Spirit, Paul built Christian congregations all over Asia Minor. He did not see his work as chore or duty, but as honor and privilege. He fondly referred to the church as "a temple"—a holy place where God's Spirit dwells.

Prayer: Master Builder, help us to see our caregiving responsibilities as holy work. That point of view can replace burned-out walls and promote a joyous purpose for our ministry to our loved ones. Amen.

123
Oh, Mama

—∞∞∞—

Scripture Reading: Psalm 16

You show me the path of life.
In your presence there is fullness of joy;
in your right hand are pleasures forevermore.

Psalm 16:11

The Meals on Wheels route went well until the seventh stop. I balanced the three-compartment Styrofoam food plate, bread, dessert, milk carton, and a couple of Hershey's nuggets in my left hand and rang the doorbell. When I looked through the clear storm door, I saw Jane lying on the floor with her legs twisted up under her. She looked straight at me with pleading eyes. I tried to open the storm door, but it was locked.

I called to Jane and motioned about going around as an option. She made an affirmative nod, and I went to the back. I found an unlocked door and entered. I called out to let anyone in the house know I was the Meals on Wheels person. Jane's daughter answered my call and met me in the hallway. I explained I could see her mother had fallen, and I was trying to get in to help her.

As we entered the living room, Edith spoke, "Oh, Mother, what have you done? What happened?"

Jane explained, "I fell out of my bed, so I scooted in here on my bottom."

"Oh, Mama, when you fall, you are supposed to push the button on this thing you wear around your neck. Why didn't you push it?"

Jane made no response. It was as if she were deaf and in her own world.

I asked Jane where her walker was, and she indicated the bedroom. I got it and then positioned myself behind Jane and lifted her up, using my knees the way home-health nurses had taught me. Edith pulled on Jane's hands, and we managed to get her to a standing position. But Jane could not lift her feet, and we had to coax her to slide her feet to the walker. When she got stable on the walker, we helped her swing her body into an armchair.

Edith's next words reflected embarrassment, helplessness, and despair. "Oh, Mama, you're wet." Again Jane made no response.

Both mother and daughter are up in years. I don't know what their relationship was like before Jane's dementia advanced to this stage, but I know Edith needs help. I had invited her previously to attend our support group meetings. She said she was coming, but she has never shown up. Perhaps she is too depressed to get herself dressed and drive to the church where we meet.

I gave her a huge hug and wiped tears from her cheeks. "Please, Edith, come with me to the next meeting. We can't help Jane, but we can help you. There's even free counseling."

Prayer: Savior and Lord, the psalmist speaks of you showing him the path of life. Please show Edith the way out of the Slough of Despair and guide her to a better understanding of her mother's illness. Bring her to peace in you. Amen.

124

Pain Pump Pains

―⊗⊗⊗―

Scripture Reading: Hebrews 12:7-11

*Now, discipline always seems painful rather than pleasant at
the time, but later it yields the peaceful fruit of righteousness
to those who have been trained by it.*

Hebrews 12:11

My husband had his "lube and oil change" this morning. That's
what he calls the trips to the pain management clinic where his
surgically installed pump is emptied and refilled with narcotics
for another two-month interval.

As I set about the hassle of getting Bob to the medical center
on time, I thought, "This pain pump is a royal pain." Friday is
supposed to be my day to stay home and write. My sullen
thoughts centered on the pump often throughout the day. I
remembered the long, involved psychological and medical tests
Bob endured in order to get approved. I recalled the doctor who
took a firm stand when the insurance company balked. He
became a determined advocate for his patient, who has suffered
with chronic pain for decades.

Those "pre-pump" years were rough. When Bob took his meds
orally, the drug had to work its way through the digestive system
into the blood stream. When he took the medicine by injection, it
had to work its way through tissue. Once the drug kicked in, he
found relief but was oversedated. He slept until the drug wore off
and the pain returned. He suffered terribly until the next pill or

shot took effect. The peaks and valleys of that roller-coaster lifestyle were extreme—highs became sedation and lows brought excruciating suffering. The pain pump immediately changed the quality of Bob's life. The little computer in his abdomen dispenses small-dosage amounts every few minutes around the clock, controlling the pain without sleepy highs and miserable lows.

There have been a few glitches. Once the pump malfunctioned and had to be replaced. Another time, the tube running from the pump up the spinal column to the stem of the brain became clogged and had to be changed. A few months ago, the original doctor closed his pain-pump practice. It took weeks to find someone who accepts Medicare patients. I shuddered at the thought of Bob going through a torturous, perhaps fatal, withdrawal. But we found another doctor in time and avoided a crisis.

Tonight I feel foolish for fussing about spending the morning at the clinic. When I began to reflect on reasons for being so peeved and angry, they seemed silly compared to the benefits of the life-transforming pump that helps my beloved get through the day. I recalled those pre-pump nights when Bob cried, "Oh, Brother Jesus; oh, Brother Jesus; oh, Brother Jesus." Thankfully, those times are gone. The lesson I learned today was that my churlish emotions are a "royal pain" too. Besides, I later found some time to write.

Prayer: Jesus, I confess I worry, fret, and slip into a foolish victim mentality with the responsibilities and interruptions of caregiving. We caregivers all have times like today. Please help us manage the little and big irritations of life better. Amen.

125

The Truth

—∞∞∞—

Scripture Reading: John 14:1-6

Jesus said to him, "I am the way, and the truth, and the life."

John 14:6a

Our associate pastor told a story as part of his sermon this week that captured my attention. I've added names in my version.

CEO Jack Atwood made the decision to retire after thirty years. He called in six executive managers and told them about his plan to retire in one year. He said he would decide his successor in an unusual way and proceeded to explain his method. He would give each manager a seed. The person who had the most beautiful, healthiest, largest plant at the end of the year would become the new CEO.

During breaks over the months, the execs discussed the progress of their growing plants. That is, all except Jim. He secured a large pot, potting soil, fertilizer, and planted his seed. He studied the right light and water requirements and did everything perfectly. But his seed did not sprout, grow, or show any signs of life. He continued to nurture and care for it, but nothing happened.

Fifty-one weeks went by, and time for the big reveal arrived. Jim did not want to take his pot in; he was too embarrassed by his failure. However, his wife told him he must take his pot and attend the meeting. Reluctantly he agreed and joined the other five managers, whose pots contained lush, green, beautifully shaped plants. Jim wondered how Mr. Atwood would be able to choose from among them. The retiring CEO stood up and made a surprise announcement. He announced Jim would take over leadership of the company in a week.

The other five were disgruntled and protested, "Jim has nothing in his pot—nothing at all." It was then that Jack Atwood told the six executive managers he had boiled the seeds. They were ruined and could never grow.

The story reminded me of the need to cultivate reality in my life, to strive for truth. Caregivers do not need to live in denial about the way things really are. Sometimes it feels like we water and tend boiled seeds. Our loved one will not be healthy and vibrant again. Life is not, nor will it ever be, the same.

Day by day we take care of our disabled family member or friend. With Jesus as CEO we can get rid of deception tailored to unrealistic expectations. All we are called to be is faithful, not successful.

———————————

Prayer: Son of God, enfold us with your Spirit, truth, and love. Amen.

126
Too Much

Scripture Reading: Galatians 6:1-5

All must carry their own loads.

Galatians 6:5

"Bob, what are you doing?"

"I'm putting the trash and recycles out."

"No, sweetie, don't do that. I'll do it as soon as I finish my prayer time. Remember last time you tried to do the trash, you fell and hurt your ribs. Please, stop."

I paused and thought about what I had said. What is this little exchange really about? I was blindsided by a sudden awareness I was taking over another of my husband's responsibilities. It struck me the two of us were sinking into a well of diseased dependency. Yes, he needs my help to button buttons, to set out meds, and to prepare meals. In addition to housework and laundry, I now do all the bills, financial tasks, and taxes. There is a crazy muddle of change in our traditional marital roles.

God is teaching me this very moment a lesson I pray I never forget: I do not have to constantly watch what Bob does and offer to do it for him. If I am hovering, I am like a sick mama. Too much automatic aid can bring on too much dependency and too much cohesiveness. There is such a thing as too much caregiving.

I do not want to overplay or to overfunction any more. I regret behaving that way with my husband. He is stronger now, and he wants to help me by taking out the trash. I call out to him, "Bob,

I think it is wonderful that you want to help me with the trash. I would appreciate it if you will continue that job. It is such a helpful and loving thing for you to do."

I resume my Bible study, but one ear listens in case Bob has problems. I have to let him try—and perhaps fail and eventually ask for help. This approach feels uncomfortable, but it is healthier. The more I let him do for himself, the more self-respect he will gain from his successes. From now on, I refuse to let his health problems give him permission to curl up and vegetate. I am not going to enable excessive dependency on his part or my part any more. I had taken over, but I am giving back every possible function my care receiver can manage. I don't want to erode his self-respect and dignity. Scripture reminds me, we bear one another's burdens, but "all must carry their own loads."

———————

Prayer: Dear God of Wisdom, I struggle to understand healthy boundaries in my role as a caregiver to my husband. I confess I have done too much at times. Grant us care providers the ability to cultivate a holy balance in our relationship with our care receivers. Amen.

127

Tribute to a Few Good Men

———∞∞∞———

Scripture Reading: 2 Peter 1:3-11

His divine power has given us everything needed for life and godliness, through the knowledge of him who called us by his own glory and goodness.

2 Peter 1:3

According to a 1998 U. S. Department of Health and Human Services survey, more than fifty million people provide care for a chronically ill, disabled, or aged family member or friend. Approximately 60 percent of family caregivers are women.

That means 40 percent of caregivers are men. Men traditionally do not bathe, feed, dress, nurse, and nurture anyone but themselves. They typically don't clean house or shop. Most male caregivers are over the age of sixty-five and adjusting to retirement at the same time they must adapt emotionally to assuming responsibility for an ill and dying spouse. The new things to cope with and learn are legion.

I have known several of these heroes. I remember them with deep respect and heartfelt admiration for their loyalty and loving devotion to their wives. I immediately think about Uncle BF, who drove across town twice a day to feed his wife in an Alzheimer's facility. He feared she would not be fed properly, so he made the trips for years. His devotion to his spouse, who didn't know him, took a huge toll on my uncle's physical and emotional heart. He died not long after she did. His experience fits the National Family Caregivers Association statistics that this level of stress can take as much as ten years off a family caregiver's life. Mortality risks for well spouses of dementia and Alzheimer's patients are even higher.

James, a kind octogenarian and member of my church, is on a journey that parallels my uncle's, except that his wife is mentally keen and alert. He goes once or twice a day to the nursing home to feed her. His devotion and self-sacrifice touch my heart.

Sam, another amazing man, managed to keep his wife with Alzheimer's at home for many years. Her diagnosis came days before his retirement, and I cannot imagine the challenging adjustments he made. One feature of Sam's pilgrimage is unique. He never let himself become socially isolated as a number of caregivers do. Even though his wife died several years ago, he continues to cofacilitate a support group that helped him during his caregiving years. He is a popular workshop speaker at forums for caregivers and leads grief-recovery seminars.

Other men I've known who have cared for a sick spouse include family friend Mr. Ed and a Meals on Wheels client in his nineties also named Ed. Three men from my church family have nursed and lost their wives to cancer in recent months.

All these husbands have two things in common: they loved their wives and they love their Lord enough to take on unfamiliar roles and do them well.

Prayer: Lord, marriage is a sacramental life to be honored and cherished. Thank you for the example of these good faith-filled husbands. Amen.

128
Thanksgiving Thanks Giving

━━◦◦◦━━

Scripture Reading: Psalm 107:21-22

Let them thank the LORD for his steadfast love,
for his wonderful works to humankind.

Psalm 107:21

After breakfast this Thanksgiving morning I hurried to my prayer chair to begin my daily devotions followed by a litany of thanks. An annual ritual of quiet time devoted to counting my blessings actually began years ago when I was adjusting to sad, traumatic changes in my life. I lay in bed at my cousin's house snuggled under warm homemade quilts and cried for what "used to be." When thoughts turned to the good things in my life, I learned an unforgettable lesson: the blessings far outweigh the negatives.

This Thanksgiving I first read an entry in a little book by Joan Chittister: "Thanksgiving is almost the hardest season of the year. Admit it: it is so difficult to be really thankful for the things we take for granted. *Thankfulness is a virtue to be cultivated* (emphasis added)—and it does not come easily to some."

Next I read these words in the devotional magazine *Forward Day by Day*: "I find it difficult to concentrate on thanking God when I am worrying. But when I can divert my attention and give thanks for my blessings, I slowly calm down. *I think it is a matter of practice* (emphasis added). If we offer thanks daily it becomes easier to offer thanks when we are anxious."

My list of blessings starts with family and friends. Then I thank God for shelter, food, little dog, plumbing, electricity, heat and air conditioning, books, and music. I give thanks for life in a great nation with freedoms to speak, worship, and follow dreams. Thoughts about the countless wonders of nature lead me to sing the Doxology: "Praise God, from whom all blessings flow."

Caregiving is difficult. Watching a loved one suffer and change is heartbreaking. But I am thankful for Thanksgiving because it forces me to pause and remember the goodness of the Lord. My personal tradition of thanks giving leads me to the number one blessing on my list. It is this: I've been loved—Father, Son, and Holy Spirit–loved. My help and my salvation are secure. No matter what.

My spiritual director shared a little story with me that seared its way into my soul. He spoke about Jesse M. Trotter, late priest and seminary professor, who was scheduled to preach at the graduation ceremony one spring. His son committed suicide a few weeks before the event, and Dr. Trotter was given the option of canceling. He chose to go forward with the schedule. That day he gave the shortest, most poignant sermon ever. He simply said, "I have been to the bottom, and I want to tell you, the bottom holds."

Knowing we are cradled in God's steadfast love, no matter what is happening in our lives, tops my list of blessings today.

———————

Prayer: Creator, Redeemer, Sustainer, may we never forget to say *thank you*. Amen.

129
The Labyrinth

───❧───

Scripture Reading: Psalm 139:1-18

*You search out my path and my lying down,
and are acquainted with all my ways.*

Psalm 139:3

Today I went to the bookcase to get the dictionary and noticed the finger labyrinth placed on the shelf. I picked it up and admired the circular pattern cut into the dark gray stone plus a small carved cross that marks the beginning (and ending) of the design. The rock fit perfectly into the palm of my left hand while I traced the path to the center with my right index finger. At the center is an empty space. I paused there for a while before tracing the path with my fingertip back out to the cross. I slowly repeated the exercise several times.

A friend introduced me to the labyrinth several years ago when she invited me to walk a large floor model at the Episcopal Church of the Transfiguration in Dallas. It is a replica of one in Chartres Cathedral near Paris. The Reverend Dr. Lauren Artress, author of *Walking the Sacred Path*, has led the reintroduction of the labyrinth as a means of spiritual practice since 1991 when she first saw the Chartres labyrinth. The Chartres labyrinth is believed to be the oldest existing labyrinth of the medieval design with its eleven concentric circles divided into four quadrants.

In medieval times walking a labyrinth approximated a religious pilgrimage—a quest with the hope of becoming closer to

God. Sometimes the walk served as an act of repentance with the repentant "walking" to the center on their knees, then rising to walk out upright, forgiven and healed.

The labyrinth, with a history steeped in Greek traditions and Gothic cathedrals, is undergoing a revival in the United States. Hundreds of hospitals, hospices, spas, churches, and schools have added a labyrinth to their facilities. In 2006 there were more than two thousand labyrinths in this country. Ten elementary schools in Santa Fe have them, and the students love the combination of quiet meditation and movement.

A labyrinth should not be confused with a maze. The labyrinth has an unambiguous route to the center and back out; it is not designed to be difficult to navigate. A maze, on the other hand, presents a puzzle in the form of a complex branching passage with choices of path and directions. You can get lost, bewildered, and disoriented in a maze. Not so in a labyrinth.

Some days my caregiving role is like a maze—a jumble of puzzling, unsettling, and disturbing choices and chores. Those days I resent my life. But today I made a journey using my finger labyrinth and achieved some contemplative moments that quieted my mind and led me to an awareness of God and a better me.

Prayer: Dear God, when we are busy thinking outwardly and feeling all alone, draw us along a labyrinthine path into our heart of hearts, where we shall find you. Amen.

130
Trust and Obey

—∞—

Scripture Reading: Proverbs 3:1-8

Trust in the LORD with all your heart
and lean not on your own understanding.

Proverbs 3:5, NIV

My husband knows I am writing this daily devotional for care-givers. He also is somewhat aware the project mirrors my own spiritual journey. Bob has lost some mental abilities, specifically number functions, but his keen intelligence and intuition have returned after two years of rehab. He was enjoying a big break-fast of bacon and pancakes when I mentioned I had tried for several hours the previous afternoon and evening to write a devotion without any success. He peered over the top of his half-glasses and looked at me with his wonderful blue eyes. He spoke, "It will be okay. Trust and obey, like we sang in the hymn yesterday."

"Trust and obey"—two little words with big demands. I don't have the same difficulty with "obey" that I have with "trust." I can easily slip into my worry mode when Bob has a bad episode, when the children don't call, when the deposit is late, or I can't find words to write. Perhaps those are the times when I confuse trust with wants, needs, and hopes. Trust has been perhaps the most difficult spiritual challenge I have faced as a caregiver. The future looks grim in the midst of this suffering—suffering for Bob and for me. Feeling confident that God is in control and all will be well can seem ephemeral. And now I've added to that struggle the audacious calling to write about this experience.

Learning to trust is a key in our relationships with others and with God. People may let me down, but the Lord God has never failed me yet. Why can't I release my worries to the Almighty and merrily bounce through each day? Even when my prayer requests are met with a holy No?

Christian counselor Marie Chapian has labeled trust in God as a "gift" in a devotional book titled *His Gifts to Me.* Total trust is not something we can force, but it comes as we meditate upon God's words and act upon them. God's presence can permeate our worrisome environments and open us to receive the gift of absolute trust in the future for ourselves and for our loved ones. Chapian's meditation on God's words about trust in scripture led her to write this poem:

> I have told you
>   to trust Me
> and safely snuggle, like a young bird
>   beneath the shadow
> of its mother's mighty wings,
>   not just for special favors,
> a worm, an insect,
>   or a miracle here and there.
> Trust Me to be *Me.*

Through all life's jolts and jollies, God has been and will continue to be with me. God is God of the mountains and God of the valleys. May I stop my silly worrying and simply follow my care receiver's sage advice to "trust and obey."

Prayer: Loving and steadfast God, you have never failed your people yet, and you never will. Grant us the wisdom to trust you always. Amen.

131

Wedding Day

Scripture Reading: Song of Solomon 2:8-17

My beloved speaks and says to me:
"Arise, my love, my fair one,
and come away."

Song of Solomon 2:10

I wished my beloved were sitting beside me in the pew watching our granddaughter Katie exchange marriage vows with a wonderful young man. Katie glowed even more exquisitely than her gown. Matt looked nervous but burst into smiles when the flower girl stopped midway down the aisle. Little Lucy stood frozen when she discovered no more rose petals in her basket. Her ring-bearer brother, the maid of honor, and the entire wedding party motioned for her to join them at the altar. When the petite child finally decided to move again, she ran forward and grabbed her brother's hand.

The ceremony was simple, traditional, and sweet. "I do" was spoken with sincerity and love, expressing hopes for the future. The applause was exuberant when the pastor pronounced them "husband and wife," and the happy newlyweds exited the University of the Ozarks chapel.

The generations had come together to celebrate the lineage and heritage that will continue to grow with this young couple. I recalled my own wedding day when I vowed to cherish my husband "in sickness and in health." I assumed we would age and decline, but I never expected the sickness to be so pervasive and challenging. Bob's chronic health problems have lasted for years now and could go on many more. The love that led me to make the vows will lead me faithfully on for as long as we both shall live.

Love in the Song of Solomon is seen as a communion of souls—an idea and an ideal. The Song shows a relationship charged with energy and a joyous, sensual world in which the land's springtime rebirth is the counterpart of the girl's blossoming into womanhood. The love is egalitarian and mutual. Both lovers desire, behave, feel, and speak with the same intensity in this poetic pastoral scene of simple pleasure and quiet.

The words of the Song of Solomon are often applied to several types of love, such as God's divine benevolence that bestows blessings on humankind, the mature sexual communion solemnized in marriage, and the human devotion that transcends death. In the Jewish tradition, the Song is a religious allegory recounting God's love for Israel. For Christians it is a parable of Christ's love for his bride, the church.

Prayer: Lord God, you are not a fair-weather beloved. You love us in our sickness and sin. May we never forget to commune with the Groom who loves us "until death do us part" and beyond into eternity. Amen.

132

Wide-Open Arms

Scripture Reading: Mark 10:13-16

*He took [the little children] up in his arms, laid his hands
on them, and blessed them.*

Mark 10:16

For several years doctors and physical therapists have worked with my husband in hopes of slowing the deterioration of his spine. He is bent almost in half now, and his medical care includes a vigorous program of manipulative posture therapy. One day when he was on the treatment table, I watched the efforts to improve his alignment and mentioned thinking I was out of alignment myself. An appointment a few days later proved that was indeed the situation, probably caused by a fall from a ladder resulting in three broken ribs several years earlier.

Every two months I go for a checkup. The clinic is part of a teaching program, and students rotate in and out every few weeks. My therapist this week was a beautiful young woman expecting her first child in five months. While she worked on my back and neck, the two of us talked about motherhood, her concerns over her husband's dangerous occupation, and the heart stuff of women. The conversation flowed into the subject of the importance of our faith in our lives.

I was lying on my back on the narrow table when Netta told me to spread my arms out to the side with palms up and let them relax toward the floor. She explained this position expanded my chest muscles and benefited my lungs. She resumed the massage and the conversation. A few minutes later she asked if she could pray for me. Without waiting for my consent, she began praying for me, my husband, and for all the caregivers who would some day read my devotional. I reciprocated with prayer for her, her husband, her unborn child, and her ministry to me and so many others.

Spontaneous praying, even with people met briefly, is not uncommon for me. But a fascinating part of the experience with Netta was the way my arms were outstretched like our Lord's on the cross. I received a powerful reminder of Christ's vulnerability and outpoured sacrificial love. I pictured Jesus blessing the little children, including Netta, her baby in utero, and her husband. Time and space blurred in Christ's presence. The treatment room became holy ground.

My life as a caregiver is mostly isolated, but it certainly isn't lonely. A loving Savior loves me at all times. His wide-open arms invite his children to extend hospitality to one another as members of God's worldwide family. No one is ever truly alone.

Prayer: Christ Jesus, the blood you poured out on the cross cleanses and unites us with brothers and sisters all over the world. Help your people who are weighted down by caregiving responsibilities to find wide-open arms of hospitality and sweet prayer-filled support. Amen.

133

Sing, My Little Dove

—✦—

Scripture Lesson: Psalm 55:1-8

I said, "Oh, that I had the wings of a dove!
I would fly away and be at rest."

Psalm 55:6, NIV

W. Paul Jones related a brief personal experience in the prologue of his book *Teaching the Dead Bird to Sing*. He lived in a third-floor apartment in an inner city near a roaring interstate. One morning he heard scratching outside his window and discovered a dove building a nest on the ledge. She had laid one small white egg in the flimsy twig birthing place.

Jones watched discreetly for fourteen days until his "grand-bird-daughter" was born. One postnatal week later, a freezing rain came. The author awoke to hear the mama bird cooing. Thinking all was well, he peeped around the window blind to find his little friend had propped up her small infant bird in the corner of the sill. She patiently repeated her cooing as she tried to teach her frozen baby to sing.

Shortly afterward, W. Paul Jones took a nine-month leave from his seminary teaching and entered a monastery to "perch on some lonely sill" until he could be "discovered by One capable of teaching me to sing an untimely song in an unlikely place."

My neighborhood has a plentiful supply of mourning doves, and the brownish gray birds often frequent the ground below the feeder outside our dining room window.

Their plaintive *ooah, cooo, cooo, cooo* tug at my sensibilities, especially when only one bird is calling. Mourning doves are monogamous and mate for life. A lone bird will sing for days hoping for a response from the beloved.

Sometimes when my husband is going through tough times, I wonder how I might handle his death. We've been tested by dramatic changes in his health and subsequently our lifestyle. We experience mountains and valleys all within one day as we bump up against vulnerability and insecurities. Yet somehow we are able to limp on toward the sacred shelter of the Holy One.

Like the psalmist, at times I feel "my heart is in anguish within me; the terrors of death assail me" (Ps. 55:4, NIV). It's interesting how I don't fret about my own dying; it's Bob's chronic pain and raw struggles that assault my spirit. A difficult lesson for a caregiver to learn is letting go and letting God. I didn't cause my husband's problems, and I certainly can't cure them.

When I sing my mournful songs to the Lord, when I feel most exposed and frozen, there is always an answer to my calls. God's response is love, hope, and grace.

Prayer: Thank you, O God, for listening to the coos of your doves. You find us whether we anguish on lonely windowsills or shout joyful praises. You are always with us. What blessed assurance. Amen.

134

Words for Bobby

—∞—

Scripture Reading: Romans 8:31-39

*No, in all these things we are more than conquerors
through him who loved us.*

Romans 8:37

Last year our son Bobby waged a fight for his life against squamous cell cancer in his neck and tonsils. The radiation burned his throat and esophagus so seriously he could not swallow. A feeding tube had to be installed. He became frightfully thin and even thinner when that equipment had to be removed after an infection developed at the feeding tube site. For months this family practice doctor and his wife, a beautiful helpmate nurse, fought the good fight.

What kind of Christmas present do you give a young couple going through a life crisis like that one? In one of my catalogs I spotted a framed print of wise words I thought might encourage Bobby and Becky:

What Cancer Cannot Do

It cannot cripple love.
It cannot shatter hope.
It cannot corrode faith.
It cannot destroy peace.
It cannot kill friendships.
It cannot suppress memories.
It cannot silence courage.

It cannot invade the soul.
It cannot steal eternal life.
It cannot conquer the Spirit.

—Anonymous

I love the remarkable effort of those words to eliminate the victim mentality. "Why me?" is never an issue, but the message focuses instead on hope, reassurance, and strength of faith. These words communicate victory, whether living in an earthly body or gone to the "new life" beyond.

Bob and I spent many weeks and months on our knees praying for our son and his family. Bobby had an army of prayer warriors in several states asking for a miracle. He studied scripture, especially the epistles of Paul, and leaned heavily on his faith, family, and church. We are grateful to report he has been declared cancer-free for almost six months. He works, runs marathons, and stays immersed in the activities and needs of his six children.

As a caregiver, I catch myself on occasion slipping into a victim mentality. "Bobby's words" are a great reminder that we can be victorious in our attitude. Other words could be substituted for *cancer*, words such as *Alzheimer's, Parkinson's, Muscular Dystrophy, caregiving*, and on and on. No matter what kind of life crisis or religious affiliation a person may or may not have, the words are designed to reassure and give hope.

Prayer: Dear Jesus, we have called on you for the healing. Come, dear Lord, and help all of us who are broken in body and spirit to gain victory in you, whether we live or die. Amen.

135
Trash Talk

—⚬⚬⚬—

Scripture Reading: Psalm 24:1-6

*The earth is the Lord's and all that is in it,
the world, and those who live in it.*

Psalm 24:1

Twice a week the city sends trucks to pick up our garbage. One day weekly a truck comes to get the recyclables. Today both trucks were scheduled to come, so I hauled the bin and bag curbside before heading to my prayer chair for morning devotions. After nestling into my sacred space, I remembered how Bob used to do the trash job. Daily he took the overflowing can under the sink and fed the big can out in the garage. Then, on the right day, he moved everything to street's edge.

Two years ago when we moved from our house and large yard to a one-story duplex, Bob had difficulty learning the new pickup schedule. Even after I posted the days on the fridge, he often became confused, and I would have to retrieve his well-intentioned good deeds from the sidewalk. Bob became increasingly unsteady on his feet and sustained several bad falls. Using a walker only made the situation worse. I finally convinced him he could help me more by not helping me with the trash. So now I do it all.

I sat and thought about the amount of trash I had deposited for pick-up—everything from potato peels to junk mail. The bags and bins are filled to the brim with the wastes of our daily existence. It is both astonishing and appalling. It pricks my conscience to be responsible personally, socially, and ecologically for this much garbage *every week*. But being responsible for a part of the landfill does not stop my frantic rush to get my psychological and physical trash out of sight and out of mind as quickly as possible. I am a human being making a human mess. Some of it is unavoidable in the same way a deciduous tree has no choice but to shed its leaves. But the real question begging my attention is: *What is excessive in my life, and how does my excess affect other human beings?*

My awareness of the importance of being a good steward of all that God has given me continually grows as I learn more about ecological issues. Everything is a gift from God. If I treat my gifts with contempt or indifference, I should rent a landfill bulldozer to scrape away the trash of a gluttonous mind and soul. Environmental stewardship and compassion for creation are not simply issues of survival. They are issues of spirituality and relationship with the Giver. Taking out the garbage is a mundane chore, but today I feel challenged to follow our Lord's precepts in my daily choices.

Prayer: Lord God, keep us mindful of what we accumulate. Grant us the ability to surrender excess. And keep us in simple harmony with the environment outside and within our homes. Amen.

136

Waiting

Scripture Reading: Isaiah 30:18-21

Therefore the LORD waits to be gracious to you;

. . . .

blessed are all those who wait for him.

Isaiah 30:18

Waiting for medical test results is horrible. Truth be told, this caregiver has little faith in these tests. A report will arrive at the doctor's office. He will phone to say nothing has changed, and Bob is doing fine. But I know otherwise. He's slowly losing ground. At support group sessions, caregivers often mention having a similar experience. Doctors rely heavily on tests, but caregivers often pick up on the subtle changes a doctor or others may not notice.

Today Bob and I are in "wait mode" to learn results from a test to show if Bob has had a stroke or seizure. This day happens to fall at the beginning of the church season of Advent (the four weeks before Christmas), a time of waiting and preparation for the Christ child. I retrieved the Advent wreath from the attic and set it out on our table.

While completing the setting with candles, Bible, and offering basket, I thought about Mary in her period of waiting. When I studied art history in college, I found one masterpiece especially intriguing—the Annunciation triptych known as the *Merode Altar-piece*, painted around 1425 by Robert Campin. A triptych consists of three separate wooden panels connected with hinges. The *Merode* center panel depicts Mary seated on the floor next to a pewlike bench in a middle-class Flemish home. Gabriel is present, but Mary has not seen him (unlike most representations in which she backs away at the sight of the angel). Here she sits calmly reading scripture. Joseph is busy in his workshop in the right panel, and the left panel depicts the triptych donor and his wife kneeling as they look through the open door.

Symbolism abounds in this oil painting, but one feature particularly stirs something deep within me. A beam of light or gust of wind comes through a window above Gabriel's head, snuffs out the candle on the table, and ends near Mary's ear. Moving along this Spirit beam is a small figure of Christ carrying a cross. Like the patrons, I feel I have been invited to Mary's impregnation with the Word. "And the Word became flesh and lived among us" (John 1:14).

Today I identify with the Mary in the Campin triptych. I sit calmly, read the Testaments, and let my heart and mind be filled with the Spirit of the Christ child. Despite the worries that accompany Bob's serious health issues, the waiting is easier. I am less anxious about test results when I lose myself in the aliveness of the "Living Word."

Prayer: Jesus, may we wait expectantly and patiently today with hope and trust you will be with us in this world and in the world to come. Amen.

137

The Funeral

───∞∞∞───

Scripture Reading: John 6:35-40

*"This is indeed the will of my Father, that all who see the
Son and believe in him may have eternal life; and I will raise
them up on the last day."*

John 6:40

Three weeks ago Miriam and I met for an hour at a neighborhood Starbucks to share our caregiver experiences. She told me
John's status had deteriorated to the point that, a few days earlier, he had been placed in hospice care at home. She described
how her husband's initial despondency was followed by complete
acceptance of the situation and a request for some fresh strawberries. We laughed. Well spouses of the chronically ill do that—
laugh at the bittersweet moments found in their pilgrimages.

Soon after learning about John's death, I delivered food to
Miriam's house. Miriam told me she and John had gone to a
movie the night before he died. "It all happened so fast," she said.
"He began to have difficulty breathing in the night. His breathing
became more and more of a struggle until I could hardly stand to
watch. He put up such a strong fight, but he became exhausted.
About one in the afternoon, John took his last breath. It was hard,
Nell, so very hard. But I am glad I was there holding his hand."

John's funeral celebrated the life of a kind, devout Christian
man. Per his request, the service was a folk Mass with guitar
music. The powerful baritone voice of the song leader filled the

church with some of John's favorite music. The minister's homily reflected the deep love and respect he held for his parishioner "who prayed much."

One of the Communion hymns was "I Am the Bread of Life." John's beautiful wife, Miriam, stood when we sang the fourth verse, which is based on these scriptures:

> Jesus said to [Lazarus' sister Martha], "I am the resurrection and the life. Those who believe in me, even though they die, will live." — John 11:25

> "This is indeed the will of my Father, that all who see the Son and believe in him may have eternal life; and I will raise them up on the last day." — John 6:40

Miriam and John's friends and family knew with quiet confidence that John had entered the gate of eternal life. He was already singing praise music with joyful abandonment all over heaven.

While driving home, I decided that I want a funeral just like John's — a celebration of God's love, grace, and mercy for a child of God "who prayed much."

Prayer: Most merciful God, grant that your servant John may rejoice in his eternal glory. Surround Miriam and his family with your love. May any who have lost a loved one not be overwhelmed by their loss but have such assurance in your goodness, they will be strengthened to meet the days ahead until they too are "raised up on the last day." Amen.

138
Dinner with Ed

—⁂—

Scripture Reading: 2 Thessalonians 2:16–3:5

*Now may our Lord Jesus Christ himself and God our Father
. . . comfort your hearts and strengthen them in
every good work and word.*

2 Thessalonians 2:16a, 17

A friend's question surprised me. He asked if I had thought about what I would do when Bob dies. Ten years ago when Bob was so seriously ill and spent eleven days in the ICU, I began to consider where I would go and decided it should be near one of the children. I imagined a beach retreat with my sister and no longer cooking three meals a day. Then Bob recovered. He has been near death many times since then and always has come back strong. I no longer expect him to die before I do, nor do I entertain ideas about the future any more.

Fran took care of her chronically ill husband for thirty-plus years. When he died in his sleep, she was shocked and unprepared. She didn't realize he was dying, and she did not tell him good-bye. She simply helped him into bed for the night as usual. Now she talks about his lengthy illness and how she never expected him to die. I'm like Fran, living each day as best I know how and oblivious to the possibility things might change. Who knows if this is denial or self-protection after the emotional upheavals I've experienced for over a decade?

A ninety-four-year-old friend cared for his wife, Olga, for years before her death last winter. Weekly he told Bob and me about going to the cemetery every day and crying over his departed wife's grave. We invited him to supper with us one evening. Ed was so charming and appreciative, we decided to issue another invitation two months later. He insisted he be the host this time, and we went to a neighborhood Italian restaurant in honor of his late Italian wife.

Ed talked steadily, recounting happy memories of jobs, friends, wife, and twin sons. I watched in disbelief as the small man ate a huge platter of food plus salad and a generous dessert. He expressed how much he'd like to do this on a regular basis.

Caregiving, by its nature, is bewildering. People handle the days after the beloved dies in a myriad of ways. It is important that caregivers look out for each other and lead a grieving friend down a healthy path. Thank goodness, some continue to attend support group meetings even after their loved ones are gone. Their "been there, done that" wisdom is immensely helpful. They are great role models who demonstrate that life after caregiving can be purpose-filled too.

Prayer: Gracious God, may caregivers who have lost their loved ones feel your nearness and find eternal comfort and good hope in knowing they are never really alone. Amen.

139
Closed Doors

⸺⸺

Scripture Reading: Revelation 3:20-21

"Listen! I am standing at the door, knocking."
Revelation 3:20a

During a workshop I attended in the 1970s, the leader passed around postcards of a painting that hangs in Saint Paul's Cathedral, London. The picture and the exercise we did with it have remained indelibly imprinted on my mind through the decades. The masterpiece, entitled *The Light of the World*, is the work of British painter William Holman Hunt (1827–1910). It depicts Jesus with a lantern standing outside a door, knocking. The leader asked us to study the picture in silence for five minutes and then take another five minutes to write down what we observed.

I noted the pointed crown symbolizing the crown of thorns and noticed the peaceful, pensive face. The golden nimbus, or halo, resembled a circle of vaporous radiant light about Jesus' head. Solid colors with sharp light-dark contrasts characterize this detailed painting filled with symbols. The closed door reminded me of the closed minds and hearts of people who are unwilling to provide hospitality to anyone on the outside, even a Messiah.

Later when we shared our notes, I quickly learned I had missed the most important symbol. The door has no handle; it can be opened only from the inside. Metaphorically, Jesus can be part of a person's life only if he or she allows him in. Today's scripture reading, a reference used for the painting, talks about hearing the knock and opening the heart to let Jesus enter to share a meal. I wonder how many times a day Christ Jesus knocks and speaks and I fail to hear. Do I listen hospitably to those who seek my attention?

I have a long-standing practice of spending time each morning with scripture, devotional meditations, and prayer. I go to my special spot in the guest bedroom and close the door. When I go to the computer corner in my bedroom to write, I also close the door. The closed door signals Bob that I am cloistered and not to be disturbed. Generally he's respectful, but when he forgets it triggers a major meltdown. Rarely is the reason for interrupting important, unless you count his real reason—loneliness. He wants loving companionship.

I find it hard to believe Jesus too wants my attention and fellowship. Oh, how he must love us to stand there at the door knocking, waiting, hoping to be invited in. This Christian God is awesome. He comes to us, wants us, and never gives up on us even when the door is closed.

Prayer: Light of the World, Prince of Peace, may we fling open the door and welcome you with exuberance to our heart-home today. Teach us how to set healthy boundaries as caregivers with personal need for closed-door time while we continue to devotedly care for our loved ones. Amen.

140

He Is Risen!

━━∞∞∞━━

Scripture Reading: Luke 24:1-12

The women were terrified and bowed their faces to the ground,
but the men said to them, "Why do you look for the living
among the dead? He is not here, but has risen."

Luke 24:5

Monday, after Easter, I noticed a small, white, plastic signboard cross about thirty inches high had sprouted in the yard directly across the cul-de-sac from our dining room window. "He Is Risen" is printed on the cross piece. At the base of the cross are the words "Better Together." The couple who own the duplex, well up in years, have numerous health and aging problems. Marty was diagnosed with bone cancer eight years ago, and husband Jack has heart disease. Both are barely mobile, but their devotion and care for each other make it possible for them to remain in their own home. A daughter lives across the street if they have difficulties.

I wondered about the story behind the lawn cross until I read an article in the *Dallas Morning News* (April 8, 2007). Bruce Fogarty, his wife, and his parents made a trip to Europe in 1984. The one place the dad wanted to visit was Normandy. He wished to pay his reverent respects, particularly to those who gave their lives in the D-Day invasion. With his father, Bruce looked out across the 9,387 white crosses marking the graves of fallen soldiers. Instead of succumbing to death, he believed, these men who had made the ultimate sacrifice for their country would live again. He regarded the crosses as symbols of Christian hope and as a testament to the glorious resurrection of Easter.

Bruce dreamed about crosses in American yards as a reminder death does not win, and as a message of Easter victory. In 2005, acting on an impulse, Bruce had several thousand little white crosses produced. Seven churches distributed 6,000 crosses that Easter. Last year 80 churches placed 25,000. In 2007 more than 200 churches from 14 denominations distributed over 50,000 crosses. This amazing ripple effect deposited one of the crosses in my neighbors' garden.

Marty and Jack are devout churchgoers, even though the effort required for them to get to worship is greater than that required for Bob and me each Sunday. Their little cross reflects their love for the Lord and serves as a reminder of the sacrifice Jesus made on the cross and the sacrifice of military men and women throughout history. Bruce is right. That kind of love cannot be contained in a grave. "He is not here, but has risen." Yes, risen indeed!

Prayer: God of Easter and new life, I pray crosses will spring up in people's hearts and minds to remind us that nothing can separate us from the love of God—nothing—not death, Alzheimer's, bone cancer, heart disease, nothing. Amen.

141

Good Night and Sweet Dreams

---∞∞∞---

Scripture Reading: John 15:9-12

*"As the Father has loved me, so I have loved you;
abide in my love."*

John 15:9

I signed my name in the register in the vestibule of the tiny Chapel of the Chimes. Cherry greeted me with a big hug and a thank-you for attending her mother's funeral.

Two years earlier I had hired this lovely, intelligent woman to work as a page at the library. The staff valued Cherry's happy spirit and amazing work ethic. The small paycheck and flexible hours helped her pay bills and spend time with her mother at the Fountains Nursing Home. The social interaction with kind colleagues at our workplace also helped her adapt to the unavoidable grief and adjustments that came with the progression of Annie's Alzheimer's.

Soon after I found a seat, two coworkers slipped into the pew next to me. My eyes came to rest on a floral spray on a stand at the foot of the light pink, gold-trimmed casket. Branches of deep green Woodwardia fern served as background for the circular design of densely clustered white and rosy pink carnations. Sprigs of delicate white baby's breath softly nestled among the ruffled mass of blossoms. The flower circle whispered to me. It whispered Love Immortal with no beginning and no end. The petals spoke to me of life that is complex, simple, joy-filled, sad, paradoxical, ever changing.

I sat beneath the gentle umbrella of eulogy, songs, and prayers. The minister offered a blessing over the body. The casket was opened and we filed by. Lifeless white-haired Annie wore a pale, pale pink dress. She cradled an old, well-loved doll at her side. I quietly told her good-bye and stepped outside into the warm sunshine.

After the funeral, people milled about the grounds of the small white clapboard chapel. Cherry ushered the nursing home manager over to meet me. In a melodic deep voice, the manager said, "The residents and staff are deeply saddened by Annie's absence. When Annie came to us, we couldn't get her to settle down at night and go to sleep. It took days to figure out what was wrong. Her agitation stopped and her serenity returned once she was allowed to perform her special nightly ritual. You see, Annie believed the other patients in the Alzheimer's unit were her children. Every night we had the pleasure of watching Annie tuck patients into their beds, kiss them on the forehead, and wish them 'Good night and sweet dreams.' Then everyone fell asleep contentedly."

———————

Prayer: Lord God and Creator, may all of Annie's children, all of your children, hear the whisper of Love Immortal that goes on eternally tucking in, kissing, and wishing each of us "Good night and sweet dreams." Amen.

142

Life to Life

—∞∞∞—

Scripture Reading: John 5:24-27

*Very truly, I tell you, anyone who hears my word and believes
him who sent me has eternal life, and does not come under
judgment, but has passed from death to life.*

John 5:24

My friend Betty called to tell me she had heard from hospice
that her father was nearing the end of his life. I met Harold when
Betty and her husband brought him to Sunday worship and coffee fellowship. Over the years he moved from independent living
to assisted living and then nursing home care. He seemed to enjoy
my visits, especially since I always brought him a gift. He savored
candies, brownies, anything sweet.

It felt strange yesterday to go empty-handed, but Harold no
longer could respond. He simply lay in bed sleeping with some
involuntary twitching and shallow, irregular breathing. His pale
skin seemed too big for the extreme thinness of his body. I patted
his hand over and over and rubbed his arm. I said my farewells
and prayed for a holy passage to the next life before gently placing a good-bye kiss on his forehead. I felt a certain kinship to the
ninety-four-year-old man who had been a gifted organist, tal-
ented artist, and dynamic engineer. After all, his wife and I had
the same name.

The hospice nurse was kind, experienced, and respectful. She
had a calm confidence that let me know she was capable of help-

ing him pass from life to life in a dignified, pain-free manner. I was glad she was the one who would be with him when he took his last breath. The vigil would not be long.

Hospice is an amazing ministry of compassion both to the one who is dying (six months or less life expectancy) and to the loved ones. The program of medical, nursing, and social services provides support and alleviates suffering for dying persons and their families. Hospice can assist with legal matters such as wills, provide emotional and family counseling, as well as offer grief workshops for survivors.

For months as a Stephen Minister for my church, I companioned two women under hospice care. Many friends and support group members also praise hospice services and recommend using them in those last months, whether the client is at home or in a facility. A widow at an Alzheimer's support group session summed up hospice ministry with this comment, "They make a beautiful passing, and they have even kept up with me afterward."

———————

Prayer: O God, we thank you for the life of Harold and others who have entered the land of everlasting peace. In your compassion, console us who mourn. Give us faith to see in death the gate to eternal life, and grant us quiet confidence to continue our course on earth, until we are reunited with those who have gone before. Amen.

143
I Bow My Knees

---◦◦◦◦---

Scripture Reading: Ephesians 3:14-19

For this reason I bow my knees before the Father, from whom every family in heaven and on earth takes its name.

Ephesians 3:14-15

When Paul wrote this remarkable letter (my personal favorite), he was imprisoned in Rome awaiting trial before Nero and waiting for the Jewish prosecutors to come with their venomous hatred and malicious charges. While under house arrest, night and day, he was chained to the wrist of a Roman soldier guard.

In 3:14, Paul writes, "For this reason I bow my knees." What is the cause or reason that makes him pray? The world is in chaos. There is division everywhere, between nation and nation, between individual and individual, within a person's inner life. Paul prays for the church to fulfill its role in God's dream for faithful people who love one another. The church is to be the instrument for carrying the message of God's love to every human being. God's plan is to unify discordant elements into one in Jesus Christ.

We discern Paul's attitude in this prayer from the words "I bow my knees." The normal Jewish posture for prayer was standing, with hands outstretched and palms upward. Paul's prayer for the church is so intense he prostrates himself before God in an agony of supplication. Some days I feel the chaos in my life, in my home, in my inner being, pushes me to the edge. Like

Paul, I fall down before God, pleading for some kind of divine intervention, revelation, or miracle.

On other days caregiving leaves me wordless. The agonized pleas will not come out of my mouth. I can't even keep my inner life from roiling long enough to find a small puddle of silent prayer. When I get into this situation, I remember a story shared by a church educator about her family's Christmas tradition. Before opening Christmas gifts, each person offers a special Christmas prayer.

One year, the last one to pray was Lauren, age three, the youngest child in the family. She looked up at the bright star on the top of the tree and then turned to her mother. She started to cry because she did not know what to do. Because she had laryngitis, she couldn't speak! Lee, who was four, went over and took his sister's hand and said, "Lauren can kneel." Lauren quickly got down on her knees and bowed her head for a long time. God undoubtedly heard that mute prayer in an extraordinary way.

Whenever words fail me, I know I can always, like that little child, kneel in humility and trust God to handle the desires of my heart.

Prayer: Lord Jesus, I invite you to dwell within and strengthen my inner being. May all of us caregivers come to know the love of Christ that surpasses knowledge and words. Amen.

144
I Wish I Were a Kangaroo

Scripture Reading: Ezekiel 34:25-30

They shall live in safety, and no one shall make them afraid.

Ezekiel 34:28b

I wish I were a kangaroo. You get to hop around and ride in a pouch. That lifestyle is both free and secure at the same time. You see, this morning I woke with an unsettled, restless feeling, and it wasn't the pizza I ate last night. Days like this arrive occasionally —days when life feels so unpredictable and yet so predictable that I want to find release and relief from it all. I dream of being free to go out to find my identity, my real identity apart from being someone's wife and caregiver. On the other hand, security in a controlled environment (without spills, expensive meds, and trips to ER) has tremendous pull. A little joey has both freedom and security. Today I want to dash to the nearest pouch.

When granddaughter Abby was a child, she loved the characters in *Winnie the Pooh*. She was so entranced by them she called her mother "Kanga" and her father "Tigger." She, of course, was "Roo." If her mother was out of sight and Abby needed reassurance, she yelled, "Kanga," and her mother responded, "Roo." This charming banter not only comforted Abby but also amused her. It amused me too.

I can't explain why I feel restless and insecure today. There is no obvious reason for this feeling of being lost in a supermarket between the string beans and cornflakes. I'm generally stable and steady, with mostly bedrock faith. But is it not the whole point of faith that each day evokes a new commitment to God, life, challenge, mystery, and to giving whatever it takes? Faith is an experience, a gift of God's activity in our lives. I guess a faith that boasts of certainty is dead.

I cry out, "Abba Kánga," and I wait. In his own experience of emptiness and God-forsakenness on the Cross, Jesus showed human beings total abandonment to vulnerability, violence, and humility. In Jesus' Passion, God embraced humanity at its deepest, darkest hour of self-surrender and revealed the supreme cost of selfless love. Then the God of surprises, reversals, and advent walked into the tomb of insignificance, meaninglessness, and emptiness. God simply raised Jesus from the dead to declare being human is important. It is in your humanness that God is found. Resurrection and salvation are gifts to those who surrender in faith.

I still want to be a baby kangaroo. You get to hop around and ride in a pouch—to be both free and secure at the same time. Perhaps freedom comes from realizing I will never be completely secure. Perhaps faith is the art of living with insecurity.

———————

Prayer: Almighty and everlasting Kanga, we are grateful you come to us in our restlessness. May each of us hear you personally whisper, "I love you, little Roo. All is well. Trust me." Amen.

145

Face to Face

—∞∞∞—

Scripture Reading: Revelation 22:1-5

*But the throne of God and of the Lamb will be in it [the New
Jerusalem], and his servants will worship him;
they will see his face.*

Revelation 22:3b-4a

Two days ago I asked Andrea how she was doing. I learned her
brother-in-law has been gravely ill. She talked about how his
family had been with him at the hospital for weeks, but they had
a difficult time finding out anything from his doctor. A nurse cor-
nered the doctor and insisted he go into the room to talk with the
family. Abruptly, without feeling, the physician said, "Dan has
lung cancer and has six months at the most." Then he turned and
left the room.

The family was shocked by the doctor's demeanor as well as by
the news. They had been there day after day, and someone could
have told them. They needed to make plans as well as find a way
to deal with troubling emotions. Andrea was angry at the disrespectful way her relatives had been treated.

I asked her how she was doing with the sad news. "I was distressed at first, but yesterday I decided to call and talk to Dan.
He told me he was ready to die. He has an awesome peace ever
since he saw the face of Jesus. How can I be sad for him?"

Death seems so uncomplicated to a Christian who believes the
promises of God. "For God so loved the world that he gave his

only Son, so that everyone who believes in him may not perish but may have eternal life (John 3:16). In a few days, weeks, months, Dan will see his Redeemer face-to-face. There is no reason for fear. He will simply be enveloped by God's loving mystery.

A song with words and music written by Dottie Rambo captures what I imagine "homecoming day" will be like. Recently Bob and I heard it sung by Sandi Patty and, as we listened, we felt the power of that amazing moment when we too shall enter into "new life." The first verse and chorus of "We Shall Behold Him" go like this:

> The sky shall unfold, preparing His entrance;
> The stars shall applaud Him with thunders of praise.
> The sweet light in His eyes shall enhance those awaiting,
> And we shall behold Him, then face to face.
>
> And we shall behold Him, We shall behold Him,
> Face to face in all of His glory.
> O we shall behold Him, We shall behold Him,
> Face to face, our Savior and Lord.*

———————

Prayer: Gracious God: Father, Son, and Spirit, grant Dan and all those who are dying a serene transition into eternal rest in you. Amen.

146
Erased It

——— ∞∞ ———

Scripture Reading: John 2:13-22

Jesus answered them, "Destroy this temple, and in three days
I will raise it up."

John 2:19

My eyes were drawn to the simple but powerful black-and-white photograph of a handsome young man with his guitar in *Mississippi* magazine. I read the advertisement. Chet Lott, son of U.S. Senator Trent Lott, had recorded a blues CD to benefit the Southeast Mississippi Chapter of the American Red Cross and support the rebuilding efforts after Hurricane Katrina.

The musician and businessman, born and raised in Pascagoula, said, "There was an eerie calm after the storm. As I looked around the neighborhood that I had known all my life, I realized that hurricane Katrina had erased it . . . our home, our neighborhood, our town. The history told by the antebellum homes, small towns, and businesses for over 100 miles was gone, but not the spirit of the people."

The CD was described as a compilation of original blues songs by Lott who, in addition to being the composer, is the vocalist and plays guitar, mandolin, and harmonica on the album. I had never heard anything about the young man but decided to support his project by ordering two copies of *Erased It*.

The lyrics of the final and title song on the album brought tears to my eyes. Lott sang: "She erased all our history. I feel like I'm gonna die." The enormity of the devastation of Katrina on the Mississippi Gulf Coast remains shocking and incomprehensible.

The night before I listened to the CD the first time, I attended an educational meeting at my church on the subject of Alzheimer's disease. Before the meeting concluded, an attractive gray-haired lady spoke up, "My husband has Alzheimer's. It is like someone takes an eraser and erases a little bit more of his mind and his identity every day."

I listened to the bluesy wails of loss expressed by a gifted musician and cried for him, for my childhood homeland and her people. But I also cried for the families and victims of Alzheimer's, a disease with no cure that promises certain death, another despicable storm that "came into town and erased all our history."

The political and religious leaders erased Jesus. But Good Friday was not the final chapter of the salvation history book. Easter morning dawned and ushered in the impossible glorious hope of eternal life. Self-offering love will always overcome erasures, today as it did in Jerusalem more than two thousand years ago.

———————

Prayer: Everlasting God, we are born anew into a living hope through the resurrection of Jesus Christ from the dead. We believe your promises will be fulfilled. Amen.

147
Daddy

Scripture Reading: Psalm 145

One generation shall laud your works to another,
and shall declare your mighty acts.

Psalm 145:4

Today is the anniversary of my father's death. I used the praise psalm above in the context of my remarks at his funeral. He taught his children a deep appreciation for nature and the works of the Great Creator's hands. He reveled for hours among his camellia plants and delighted in each winged creature that graced his well-stocked feeders. One of our last conversations occurred as we sat one morning in the big rockers on the back porch watching the hummingbirds and chickadees while we sipped from mugs of hot coffee. He spoke calmly, "I know my days are numbered, but that's okay, because I have made peace with my Maker."

My thoughts about my father this morning are not really a trip down memory lane or some kind of eulogy, but instead they have prompted a reflection about my mother, his caregiver. Thirty-eight years before Daddy's death, a life-threatening viral infection left him with permanent heart damage. He developed bleeding ulcers, high blood pressure, you name it. Many times my mother experienced the emotional roller coaster of having a spouse nearly die, only to have him recover. Little did I know the costs she paid as my father's caregiver, but I can appreciate them now.

I remember my father having one terrible spell of near-death when Mother called 911. Daddy had told my mother repeatedly he did not want emergency care, resuscitation, or any of those life-prolonging procedures. He was furious with her later when he was well enough to know she had phoned for help, and the paramedics had brought him back to life. He was truly angry because he was prepared and wanted to die. She was in a terrible bind as his caregiver—wanting to honor his wishes, responsible for his well-being, and unsure about life without him. I too live in that tension.

My sister was with our parents during Daddy's final days in the Veterans' Hospital. He finally received the peace he longed for. Apparently his transition became an experience of being on holy ground for the two women at his bedside. They learned God was present with them in that sacred experience when Daddy winged his way to his Creator.

Prayer: Lord God, Lord of Life and Death, when we recall the passing of our loved ones, we feel such a sense of loss. Yet you remind us that love reaches beyond the touch of death. Treasures of memories endure the anniversaries of days like today. Grant joy and peace to all the holy dead and to those who gave them the gift of Love and Care on their journey to you. Amen.

148
Butterfly Wings

⸺

Scripture Reading: 2 Corinthians 5:17-21

So if anyone is in Christ, there is a new creation: everything old has passed away; see, everything has become new!

2 Corinthians 5:17

I wait for someone to ask the question, but no one ever does. I have expected a curious type to inquire: "After all these years, what has surprised you most about caregiving?" I have an answer. The by-product to blow me away has been the unfolding spiritual dimension of this pilgrimage for both the caregiver and care receiver. Spiritual does not mean some pie-in-the-sky, hand-holding-with-Jesus walk around the flower garden. It is the journey of the heart and soul to know the core meaning of life—to know who you are and what gives you value.

The process can be ugly and great, heart wrenching and joyous, sad and humorous. It took time for me to remove my mask. I wanted to be the efficient, compassionate, quintessential caregiver. I have learned there is no such animal—certainly not me. This is tough stuff; I stub my toes every day. Simultaneously, Bob and I are going through metamorphosis with mysterious stages like those found in the life cycle of a butterfly.

When I see a monarch flitting about my butterfly bush, I forget this creature is the result of a long journey. The flight stage is the final statement. It all starts with tiny, or microscopic, eggs. Newly hatched caterpillars are little eating machines that grow by more than a thousand-fold in two to four weeks. A caterpillar sheds its skin an average of five times. It becomes a pupa camouflaged to resemble part of the plant where it is fastened. The transformation, during the week or so of this stage, is truly a miracle. Upon emergence, the swollen body begins to pump fluids into the tiny shriveled-up wings. Within a couple of hours the wings become full size, dried, rigid, and capable of flight.

Our lives in the caregiver/care receiver relationship have stages and a complex time line that varies for each of us. We are learning that adaptation and patience are keys to metamorphosis, keys that cannot be manipulated or rushed.

I am reminded of a story from Anthony de Mello's book, *One Minute Wisdom:*

The Master always left you to grow at your own pace. He was never known to "push." He explained this with the following parable:

"A man once saw a butterfly struggling to emerge from its cocoon, too slowly for his taste, so he began to blow on it gently. The warmth of his breath speeded up the process all right. But what emerged was not a butterfly but a creature with mangled wings.

"In growth," the Master concluded, "you cannot speed the process up."

———————

Prayer: Risen Lord, help us grow into new creatures with healthy butterfly wings for our flight Home. Amen.

149

Paperwork

—⟨∞⟩—

Scripture Reading: Ephesians 2:1-10

For we are what he has made us, created in Christ Jesus for
good works, which God prepared beforehand
to be our way of life.

Ephesians 2:10

"Nell, we need to talk."

The tone of voice indicated my husband had something serious on his mind. I took a seat on the sofa next to his recliner and leaned forward to listen.

"I am dying, and I want you to have me cremated."

"Bob, you signed papers ten years ago to participate in the Willed Body Program at the medical school. Have you changed your mind?"

"Oh, that's right; I forgot. But they probably won't accept my body. I have too many diseases to qualify now. You better check and see if I can still be a donor."

"Bob, even if they accept your body, they cremate the remains. There'll be some ashes either way. Tell me what you want me to do with them."

"I don't care. Just keep them with you wherever you are."

"Do you remember the incredible valley of bluebonnets we found during our last trip to the Hill Country?"

"Oh, yes, the most beautiful place in the world."

"We felt we had entered holy ground when we turned the bend

in that old dirt road. There below us was the overwhelming beauty of masses and masses of blue flowers dancing with abandon in the springtime sun. That scenery made an imprint upon our souls. How would you feel about my taking your ashes there?"

"Nell, that sounds perfect. I like it. But please call the medical school and check on my willed body status anyway."

I did. Our names were in the registry, but the clerk wanted to mail us some new forms to update our information. Just what I needed—more paperwork. I already carry a purse big enough to accommodate a packet of papers. The large envelope holds an updated list of Bob's medicines plus living will, medical power of attorney, and "Do Not Resuscitate" forms. Copies are on file with the hospital and doctors. MedicAlert papers, medical records, and files of forms are crammed in one side of the guest room closet.

During every support group session, experienced caregivers encourage members to "preplan everything, including funeral details. Make sure your paperwork is done."

Prudent planning is great advice. But this caregiving pilgrimage often brings a series of surprises. I feel like a moviegoer watching a film about predictable unpredictability. Many times I don't understand how the story pieces fit together and why things happen the way they do. Yet I expect it somehow to make sense in the end. I simply trust the Great Filmmaker to astound me with a delightful ending.

Prayer: Great Creator God, I can imagine no more glorious way to end our script than standing amongst bluebonnets, weeping and celebrating, as we give our loved one back to you. But we caregivers know that the paperwork is in your hands. Thy will be done. Amen.

150
God's Garden

———⬦———

Scripture Reading: Jeremiah 31:10-13

*Their life shall become like a watered garden,
and they shall never languish again.*

Jeremiah 31:12

A high school classmate sold her ranch in Montana and moved to north Texas to be near her two daughters. Bobbie's husband had died the previous year, and she has been dealing with major life transitions. We talked about my coming to see her new home and having lunch together. My husband was in a period of stable health, so we arranged the date.

During our visit we discussed Neil's illness and last days. After a long hospitalization in a city miles from the ranch, Bobbie and her family made the painful decision to take her husband off life support. A family friend came with a comfortable, spacious RV and took Neil home. He spent his last five days under hospice care on his beloved ranch.

Bobbie described an episode during Neil's last hours. He opened his eyes, gazed at her tenderly, and mouthed, "Thank you. I love you." Those remarkable moments are indelibly planted in her heart, and she marvels at the gift of their "mini-reunion." I've heard other caregivers tell about the blessing of a lucid exchange with a loved one at the time of final parting.

With tears in our eyes, I took the funeral bulletin from Bobbie's extended hand. She wanted me to read the poem printed alongside a picture of her husband. She and her daughters searched through numerous books of quotations at the funeral home.

Nothing was satisfactory until they found "God's Garden." She gave me permission to share it.

> God looked around His garden and found an empty place.
> He then looked down upon this earth, and saw your
>   tired face.
> He put His arms around you and lifted you to rest.
> God's garden must be beautiful, He always takes the best.
> He knew that you were suffering, He knew you were in pain.
> He knew that you would never get well on earth again.
> He saw the road was getting rough and the hills were hard
>   to climb.
> So He closed your weary eyelids, and whispered, "Peace be
>   thine."
> It broke our hearts to lose you but you didn't go alone,
> For part of us went with you the day God called you home.

I hope you caregivers, whether your loved one is alive or dead, realize you belong to a worldwide community of remarkable people. Loving service is the law of heaven. You are followers of the World's Greatest Giver. With love there is continuous ministry in every action, even in rest. Anoint each day by sharing your great power to love and to help others. I hold you in my heart and in my prayers. You are not alone.

Prayer: O Lord, bless my family of caregivers and their loved ones. Amen.

Notes and Permissions

This page constitutes a continuation of the copyright page.

56   Charlotte van Stolk, "I Am a Coin, Gamble on Me," from *The Living Church* (1989):9. Used by permission of The Living Church Foundation.

75   Excerpt from *Splinters in My Pride* by Marilee Zdenek. Copyright © 1979 by Marilee Adenek. Published by Word Books. Used by permission. Excerpt from *Reaching for Rainbows*. © 1980 Ann Barr Weems. Used by permission of Westminster John Knox Press.

77   Based on the account by Andy Simmons, "Loving Memory," in *Reader's Digest* (November 2007):150–53.

83   Quotation from Joan D. Chittister, *The Psalms: Meditations for Every Day of the Year* (New York: Crossroad Publishing Company, 1996), 127. Excerpt of "A Prayer to the God Who Fell from Heaven" from *The God Who Fell from Heaven* by John Shea © Argus Communications 1979. Used by permission of the author.

84   Story based on one found in Marc Gellman, *Does God Have a Big Toe? Stories About Stories in the Bible* (New York: HarperCollins Publishers, 1989).

88   Lyrics by Stuart K. Hine, "How Great Thou Art," © 1953, renewed 1981 Manna Music, Inc.

92   Poem generally attributed to John Paul Moore.

93   See Harold S. Kushner, *When Bad Things Happen to Good People* (New York: Shocken Books, 1981), 110–11.

96   Excerpt from *Splinters in My Pride* by Marilee Zdenek. Copyright © 1979 by Marilee Adenek. Published by Word Books.

108   Quotations from Marianne Williamson, *The Gift of Change: Spiritual Guidance for a Radically New Life* (San Francisco: HarperSanFrancisco, 2004), 245, 251.

115   Lyrics to "If I Were a Rich Man" written by Sheldon Harnick for the Broadway musical *Fiddler on the Roof*.

128   Quotation from Joan Chittister, *The Psalms* (Crossroad, 1996), 130. Quotation from *Forward Day by Day* 73, no. 4 (November 2007 – January 2008):23.

129   Information about the labyrinth partially based on Kathleen Parrish, "The Path of Peace," *Better Homes and Gardens* (August 2006): 222, 224.

130   Excerpt from *His Gifts to Me* by Marie Chapian © 1988. Used by permission of Bethany House, a division of Baker Publishing Group.

133   W. Paul Jones, *Teaching the Dead Bird to Sing: Living the Hermit Life Without and Within* (Brewster, MA: Paraclete Press, 2002), xi–xii.

146   Excerpt from "Erased It" from the CD *Erased It* by Chet Lott © 2006 Augustus Hill Records, LLC. Used by permission of Chet Lott.

148   Anthony de Mello, *One Minute Wisdom* (Garden City, NY: Doubleday & Company, 1986), 167.

150   Poem attributed to Lindsey Zacher; www.poemhunter.com/poem/god-called-you-home/